For ~~[name]~~

11-12-17

D1240370

HEART OF A
CHAMPION

A Championship Drive Novel

SARAH BETH AUBREY

May you have the
Heart of a Champion

Sarah
Beth
Aubrey

PRAISE FOR *CHAMPIONSHIP DRIVE*

I wanted to let you know that I loved, *loved* the book. I am not the reading kind but your book hooked me. Are you thinking about writing a sequel? -- *Jordann*

What a great book! This brought back a ton of great memories for me and makes me miss traveling around to all the shows! Thanks to Sarah for having the courage and determination to write a novel and hopefully many more to come! -- *Lesley*

The storyline was telling and sincerely accurate and left you wanting for more. The premise of the fractious beginnings is a compelling family tale all too common, and many will be willfully intrigued from cover to cover. Congratulations and well done my friend. -- *Chris*

Read this! If it gives you goose bumps and you feel the thrill, excitement and can envision the walk and the ring...you need to purchase *Championship Drive* by Sarah Beth Aubrey! Thank you Sarah for the Novel! -- *Linda*

Just finished reading *Championship Drive*.......LOVED IT!! So much fun to read a book related to our "cattle lives" for once! Definitely didn't see the ending coming the way it did! When does #2 come out? -- *Kylee*

I just finished my copy of *Championship Drive*, I can't wait to see what the sequel has in store! Great job Sarah! You have a wonderful talent! -- *Trisha*

Please make a sequel to this book I love it so much I have read it at least 10 times already! I love your book! -- *Samantha*

Great job on your first book! I got it out of the mailbox Saturday night and finished it first thing Sunday morning. I can't wait to find out what happens next. Keep them coming! -- *Amanda*

Read your book and really enjoyed it. Learned a little about the high roller cattle people. I think I understand your cattle showing now. Love your book and waiting for next one. -- *Debbie*

Finally had time to read your book! Thoroughly enjoyed it*!* -- *Sherry*

For Cary,

I'm grateful for every day we walk the tan bark together.

ILU. SSW.

AUTHOR'S NOTE AND ACKNOWLEDGEMENTS

Dear Reader:

Welcome to Book Two in the *Championship Drive* series!

Wow! What an overwhelming response to *Championship Drive*. It's because of your enthusiasm for my first 'showmance' novel that I now proudly present the much-anticipated sequel that you are about to enjoy, *Heart of a Champion!*

Please remember, *Championship Drive* and *Heart of a Champion* are works of fiction and the views and observations described in the stories are solely my own. As a fiction writer, I capture interesting (and aren't there many!) aspects of the stock show industry, filtered through the lens of my own experience, and craft stories for your indulgence.

As I did in *Championship Drive,* I wish to thank the livestock showing industry, its fine people, so many that I am proud to call friends, who, with their unwavering dedication to excellence and ever-present optimism strive to make the championship drive every time they load the trailer. It's a great way to play, both in livestock and in life! I'm grateful for your inspiration.

As Cary, I, and our own crew always say, cheers to **showin', sellin', and winnin'**! (**#SSW**)!

Sarah Beth

Sarah Beth Aubrey, May 2017

DO YOU HAVE THE HEART
OF A CHAMPION?

Anyone who has ever admonished that 'winning isn't everything' must not know the sheer feeling of euphoria, the addictive taste of that first win in the ring. If they did, they wouldn't mean it, at least not *really*.

Now then, we all know that winning, that nanosecond when *we know we have won*, isn't near all that goes into it. Not even close. Playing to win, to make the championship drive, takes a lot of money, time, support of family and crew, the acceptance of friends, partners, and spouses, and a constant willingness to give your all and know you might still fail. Often. Spending countless hours getting one ready takes guts and a love of livestock that people who don't know animals just cannot comprehend.

You see, it's never truly easy to win, even for the experienced, even for those that we might perceive to have more money, more talent, or more 'politics' than we do. For everyone who raises 'em and shows 'em, I believe that the exact moment when the judge doffs his cowboy hat and extends a hand, or when a calf's rump is slapped, or when we see the dramatic point in our direction, the sense of satisfaction is the same for all of us. When we get that nod, whether it is at the county fair or the National Western, we all feel it: excitement, joy, *pride*.

Winning, or at least the quest to win and to be your very best, takes *heart*.

The Heart of a Champion.

PART ONE

GOING WEST

PROLOGUE

A Ranch in Montana, Spring 2000

I t was a move he'd done a million times. The tsk-tsk sound the blades made as he whisked them against the soft faded denim of his Wranglers. It was automatic, yet comforting, the way the blades signified a pause, a moment to reflect, a time to breath, to wipe the coarse red or white hairs away from the top of a shoulder, the center of her spine, or the curve of her belly. Wiping his shears meant he'd stepped back a beat and could think about what to do next. Problem was, last couple months, reflecting only hurt. Viscerally.

As the cow baled out of the head gate, he wiped cold sweat off his brow and feathered his hair off his forehead. Over the winter it had grown long-ish and hung just a bit on his collar now. His cobalt blue eyes squinted only slightly against the western mountains; the sun was already weak though it wasn't yet evening. For late spring it was still chilly. He hated the cold this late in the year and wondered how these cowboys could stand living in such a beautiful but harsh place where baby calves could still get frosted ears in early June.

The man arched his back, stretching out the kinks, and then reached for the can of WD-40 he always had handy for his blades. Shearing cows dulled blades in a hurry; it was a nightly ritual to oil and sharpen them before the next day. A beer would have been nice, but he couldn't risk letting the other guys on his crew start drinking before quitting time or they'd get too slow and start jacking around. Working as the boss of cow shearing team meant being paid by the head so he meant to punch as many cows through the chutes a day as possible. Letting his somewhat lackadaisical crew lose focus would mean a couple more days and no more money.

What's holding the next cow up? He wondered irritably. *Damn it, I'm getting too old for this.* A job he'd never really liked he was now starting to hate.

But at this point, for the first time in his life, he really hated about everything, especially the nights in Montana. He was drinking too much but it was about the only thing that helped him fall asleep, though lately, even that extra whiskey by his bedside couldn't coax sleep to stay. Instead, with the cold Montana moon for company, he'd lay in that hard bunkhouse bed looking out at the icy mountains and *she* would be there. At first he would just feel her presence and then she would appear, her face watery and cool against the night's backdrop. Sometimes, he tried so hard to push her away that he got pissed and yelled out inadvertently, waking up one of the other crew, but she would just fill his mind and stay, unsmiling and beautiful, close yet out of reach. Then there were the nights when he gave in to the thoughts and tried desperately to harness again the beauty of her face, the grace of her collar bones as he lay beside her those few times, to will her to take his call, to call him, to ask somebody about where he was, but then, she'd simply seem to slip away. Like a ghost, like a cold breath of air, she'd evaporate and the room would be still. He'd be left awake and alone.

All this misery is my own damn fault.

He'd screwed it up and he knew it. Since January, there had been nothing. *Nothing.* He was beginning to fear that he was crazy or that he was in love with a woman that hadn't even been real. But she had; Savannah

Morgan had been so real and the feelings he had for her when he drove out of Denver that ill-fated day had only intensified since.

He had to get her back, had to prove to her that he was worthy of her love and forgiveness. She needed to believe he was sorry. So far calls, a couple of cards, and even flowers didn't help. He wanted nothing so bad as to simply see her, but enough time had passed that he figured she wouldn't want to see him and he just kept making excuses not to go. More than once he had almost quit the ranch and gotten in the truck to drive all night to Indiana, but he just hadn't. He was too afraid of her rejection now and he knew it. Besides, right now he had nothing to offer. He was just another jerk shearing cattle somewhere in the West.

Especially after they way they'd left it, he couldn't just walk back into her life and demand she accept him; she deserved more and he wanted to be more.

Something had to change. He was seriously loosing it in all the space of the Big Sky of Montana and her long, chilly nights. Maybe there was an option for something different - either a way to forget her or change his life so she would forgive him. There was a letter sitting on his bedside table in the bunkhouse that he hadn't yet answered. When he quit the Bow String Ranch in January, he'd sworn off working for rich guys and fitting their show stock, but he didn't have any other skills and if he didn't do something different, he was going to go insane from loneliness. He just wasn't sure he could look out at that vast horizon another day while her face just kept taunting him, rising like mist of the mountains and shimmering in the prairie grass.

Cade Champion decided to take the offer in California.

ONE
LIVING LIKE A LOCAL

Central Indiana, Late Summer 2000

'*T*radition. Excellence. Quality. *Those are the words that embody the Pedrocelli Ranch.*'

"That's real original," grumbled Savannah Morgan aloud as she rubbed her eyes and set down her new laptop. She was sitting in the shade of the porch on a pleasant-for-July afternoon working on her latest writing project, an article for a cattle breed magazine about a beautiful old ranch. She was grateful to be doing the freelance writing project and the calls with one of the ranch's owners had been enjoyable, but it was hard to find something interesting to say about a place she'd never been and a lifestyle she could only imagine.

It was late afternoon, about the time one started to ponder a cold beer and heading out to start chores anyway when the phone rang. Right on cue the noise gave her pause. Ever since spring whenever the house phone rang she would stop in her tracks....

"*I need to just cut the cord on that thing and use only my cell.*" Savannah mused aloud, recovering herself. "*I wonder if it will ever come to that?*"

Savannah grabbed the phone anyway, knowing she had to stop being afraid to hear it ring. The caller ID displayed Oklahoma City, Oklahoma.

"I have got the surprise of a lifetime for you, Savannah! You are going to be soooooo excited!" her friend Macy Rawlings, a fashionable and wealthy Oklahoma oilman's daughter, gushed into the receiver. She loved Macy, but every time she called it was *always something* exciting. Savannah wasn't excited about much these days.

"In a TOTAL coincidence, Stetson told me he is trying to get the owner of Kingsley Estate Winery in Napa into the Angus cattle business and it just so happens that said owner is *literally* the sister of the woman you've been interviewing for that article on the Pedrocelli Ranch!" Macy exclaimed, barely pausing for a breath. "How cool is that? Total coincidence, huh?" she added again for emphasis.

That was quite a coincidence, Savannah mused. Monica Pedrocelli had mentioned that she and her sister co-owned the ranch, but that was about it. Still, Savannah couldn't exactly match up the relationship.

"Okay, hold on. So, why would a winery lady want to get into Angus and how did Stetson figure out that her sister with Herefords is working with me?" Savannah asked, though she knew Stetson could sniff out a rich investor better than anyone in the seedstock industry.

"Oh, you know my honey, Savvy, he's the best at finding out who's got money burning a whole in their pockets."

Savannah smiled to herself and opened the fridge while Macy prattled on. "I guess something about the fact that she has a fellow winery friend out there that has Angus – her name is Francesca Kingsley, by the way - and so anyway this Francesca lady found out about Stetson. Apparently, she thought it would be a good idea to get into the show cattle business. Well, you know, I 'spose she gets it and all since she did grow up on a ranch. Besides, then she told Stetson she wants her boys to know more about showing cattle like she did when she was a kid."

It was starting to add up. "Yeah, okay. But, still, what does that have to do with me?"

"Oh! That's where me being the best buddy you'll ever have comes in! So, she tells Stetson about the ranch she owns and Stetson is like 'isn't that the ranch Savvy is doing a story about' and I say 'yeah'. So, he gets *me* on the phone with her and I told her about you doing the article and we figure out you are working with her sister and she said –and you just gotta love the way these rich people talk – 'Well, Darling Monica didn't mention it, but an article is a lovely idea' – and then she was all like, 'bring your friend out when you visit.' Can you believe that?" Macy finished, clearly proud of the offer.

"Wow! That would be neat to see the wine country, but I couldn't get away for something like that-"

Macy had already anticipated her objections. "It's going to be *paid for*, Savvy. They have a guesthouse in the vineyard! And, you love wine! This will be so awesome!"

"I mean, it sounds so fun, Macy, and seeing the ranch would really help the piece, but I really can't think about getting away this summer," Savannah could hear Macy pouting through the phone. "I would love to, I really would, but I can't possibly go. Who would take care of things?"

"I thought you had a partner and an investor now, Savannah?" Macy was incredulous. "You've got men working for you now, girl, not the other way around!"

Savannah considered it with a little smile. It was true she had offered her old friend and neighbor, Eddie Quiggly, a percentage of the sales back in the spring and since then he had been working a lot harder than his previous level of effort. Clint Cascade, a friend she had made in Denver, had bought into her pen heifers and though he lived on the East Coast, he continued to drop by from time to time. His money was certainly helping out with the bills, especially once she sold him half interest in her Denver Champion, Tiara. At mid five-figures, the amount was definitely enough to keep the wolf away from the door for a while. Despite winning Grand Champion and selling her stock high, the Denver show back in January had been a disastrous, heart breaking experience. Coupling that with coming home to clean up her personal life and finances, she still felt as if she were barely catching her breath. She couldn't just pick up and leave. But, putting Macy off with a practical consideration wasn't ever useful.

"I don't even know what people wear in California!" She exclaimed, trying a different approach.

"It's not like its L.A. or something weird like that, Savvy. It's *wine country*," Macy said, drawing out the phrase in her Oklahoma twang. "Wear something Napa Valley cool," she finished, as if that explained it.

"Napa Valley Cool. Really? Macy, I do not know what that means and I literally have nothing to wear!"

"Girl, we are leaving in two weeks so it's time to get ready, I'll bring plenty of cute dresses to share, though they will hang off your narrow ass!"

"Macy! I would still have to shop and get feed and talk with Eddie about things and I just am not-"

"Did I mention they are flying us in a private yet?"

"Okay, maybe I'll think about it."

———— • ◆ • ————

Savannah approached the barn and breathed in the pungent scent of freshly stacked hay. The third cutting had just been put up the evening before, something evidenced by the scrapes and rashes on her wrists since she'd forgotten to wear a long sleeve when she bucked bales, but it was a gratifying feeling to know there was enough put up in squares for winter hand feeding around the showbarn.

The early evening light pitched off of the slats of barn wood and the chaff tinkered down slowly from the loft in the hazy light. It was probably going to rain tonight or by early morning, so she'd need to shut the loft doors. Hopefully the hay had cured enough in a day and a half not to be dangerous. She'd known far too many people with barn fires from hay that wasn't cured before they locked the barn up tight.

"You riding with me to watch the Grand Drive tonight?" Savannah asked as Eddie strolled up, interrupting her reflection.

Eddie Quiggly removed his grubby ball cap and itched his bald head while he employed his tee shirt to wipe his sweaty lip. Savannah looked away; Eddie's belly exposed was not a pretty sight. "Nah, I, uh, think I'd better drive myself," he said shifting a bit and acting funny.

When Savannah raised a brow at him he continued. "Well, you know, I might want to run down to that bar over there and might stay later than you would want, so, I-"

Savannah cut him off. "No problem, Eddie, just offering." She continued on.

"Who's gonna win it this year? I 'spose the Gleasons will be in the hunt anyway," Savannah answered her own question by referencing the local family that had dominated the county steer show for a decade.

"Yeah, I expect. It's a county fair; same stuff, different year."

Savannah nodded.

"Hey, uh, since we don't have anything in the showbarn, you don't mind if I head out now do ya?" Eddie asked.

Savannah waved goodbye to her old friend and turned to start feeding. It was strange not to have anything in the showbarn. Eddie was right; it did really lighten the workload in the summer and fall since there were no new calves to start breaking. She and Eddie had decided that any calves that weren't show quality were being shipped or saved back for replacement heifers. Despite his shortcomings – mostly in terms of being grouchy and not an early riser - Savannah was extremely grateful to Eddie for his help. Their alliance had kept things going around Morgan Cattle Co. as Savannah sorted through the mess of her Dad's passing, her finances, and worst of all, her failed romantic relationships. Eddie had made some mistakes, but without him Savannah might not have held it together. Now, it was good just to have someone to talk through the decisions she was making, especially the tough choice to market most of the spring calf crop over the scales.

Worried as she was, out at the county fair earlier that day, watching the Hereford steer classes had convinced her that she had made the right move. Savannah had winced when she saw a couple of the steers her dad had sold neighbors the fall before. It wasn't that the families weren't trying hard, most were, but it was just that the quality wasn't there. They weren't the kind of stock she wanted to raise and from now on she wasn't going to keep calves back that weren't good enough. Not that she didn't want county fair-level customers - she did - youth programs were the life blood of the seedstock and club calf industries, but it was more about quality and pride. With Harlan Morgan gone nine months she was beginning to see things clearly and changes she wanted to make emerged every day. The steers he had sold should have just been marketed for freezer beef or across the scales. Quality and attention to the winner's circle were going to be her hallmarks - the hallmarks of Morgan Cattle Co.- going forward!

It was especially odd to think she wouldn't be showing at Kansas City or Louisville in the fall. The fall shows just weren't feasible with the stock they had and it didn't make sense to show 'just to show'. The last year had forced Savannah to grow up in many ways. She had come to consider herself a serious breeder and wanted to be seen as such. She would take stock out when they looked right!

It was just as well she wasn't going. The last show she attended had just about killed her! Well, she hadn't died, but her heart had been broken which had to feel worse than death. Savannah had sworn off cowboys and their showing antics.

The man at fault was Cade Champion, a man she didn't intend to see ever again.

Savannah leaned on the green metal gate that gave on to the country fair show ring, careful not to brush her top against the dusty bars as the big overhead fans stirred her hair. The evening was predictably hot and humid on account of the thunderstorm that had blown through in the late afternoon. The breed champion steers were beginning to assemble at ringside while an old man, the same local volunteer that had emceed the beef show since Savannah's dad was in 4-H, announced the names of the youth and their parents into the microphone of an ancient and crackly PA system.

A well-known hog jock named Jed Hughes was judging, so his thoughts on the steers were consternating most everybody standing around that thought they knew how he *ought* to be placing them. Savannah had gone to college with Jed and had to admit he couldn't see soundness in cattle very well. She snickered to herself that his eye hadn't improved much from their judging team days.

Savannah reached up and dabbed a bit of perspiration away from her hairline just as she heard her name called.

"Hey, there, Savannah!" Jed began, approaching her rather than entering the ring. The move caused stares from a number of locals standing in her vicinity; it was pretty unorthodox for the judge to chitchat with spectators, especially right before the final drive. Savannah shifted uncomfortably as Jed reached out for a hug. She didn't have a steer in the drive, but someone was bound to complain about fairness or politics despite that fact.

"I was hoping I'd see you here! A guy has to move fast where you're concerned, huh?" Jed said.

What is going around about me? Savannah wondered with irritation.

"I didn't figure you would be to up to date on my life, Jed. We haven't seen each other since college," she said with a tight smile.

"Oh, I know, I know, but, well you see, everybody was talking at the judging team alumni banquet back in March that you had been with some older steer-jock guy in Denver, but it didn't work out but that was great news because since you finally dumped that local guy and so you were totally on the market again," he said, looking a little sheepish, but hopeful, as we pulled a hand towel from his back pocket and wiped his brow.

Savannah hadn't known Jed to judge to many beef shows, but obviously someone had told him to bring a towel to wipe the paint off his hands from handling the steers. However, it was also pretty obvious that he hadn't judged many steer shows since he didn't think twice about using that same towel to wipe his forehead, a move that left a broad streak of black paint smeared across his face. Savannah smiled sweetly and decided not to mention it.

"Is that what everybody was saying?"

"Yep. That's about it. Well, that and you were still looking good," Jed added with a toothy grin. He adjusted his soft belly over his Wrangler Riata slacks and attempted to smooth his sweaty Polo Ralph Lauren button down shirt.

He actually thinks he is scoring some points with that line? Savannah grimaced.

Seeing her pained expression, he was suddenly unsure of the rumors he'd mentioned. "Wait, uh, 'ya are divorced, right?"

Savannah *hated* that word. "Yes, I am definitely not with Troy Howell anymore," she remarked stiffly. This conversation was over. "Hey, you've got a line of steers waiting on you, better get back in there!" she added and turned away, leaving the hog guy to wonder if he might still have a shot.

As the steers filed into the line up and Jed took far too long walking them for dramatics sake, Savannah's mind wandered to the regrettable place it always did about this time in the evening - to thoughts of Cade Champion.

Falling in love was a horrible thing. Plain and simple. The term falling was a perfect name for it, too, Savannah had decided over the recent months of self-imposed nunhood. Though nearly eight months had passed since she had seen Cade Champion, she pictured him every single day. She wished he would just fade away, but he hadn't and she was beginning to get used to the company of his virtual presence. Sometimes she tried to push the thoughts aside in anger, other times she just let them float around with her like a ghost. Cade had become a sad, unattainable presence that wouldn't exactly leave and it was gloomy company. Savannah spent more time than she would ever admit to anyone dissecting 'the Cade Disaster' as she had taken to calling it. Had she fallen in love with him, yes, that was certain –painfully certain. But, did she still love Cade now? That she really didn't know. What she knew was the constant little seepage of thoughts about him now made her feel lonely and sometimes just angry. She felt hamstrung by the fact that she'd let him into her life in the first place.

Their romance in Denver had been brief, intense, and incredibly sensual. It was also a relationship with the wrong man at the wrong time and though she knew she had kept a secret from him, she was also convinced he had ruined any shot they might have had at a long-term relationship; but even that notion had been stupid, she realized. Though they talked from the day they met about a future together, she had been naive enough to believe that words from a smooth talking older cowboy could mean a damn thing. Now, here she was, back at home – and alone. She didn't have Cade and she was working very, very hard with the daily mantra that she didn't *want* Cade, either. So far so good, she thought. Though he waited far longer than he should have (that was for certain!), he actually had tried to contact her; he had called and he had written a couple letters, and he had sent flowers, but she had rebuffed it all. That stuff was easy. If he had really wanted her he could have tried harder- come to her-but he never did. So, she would force herself NOT to want him. She would will Cade Champion out of her mind no matter how long it took.

Cade had taught her one thing-never trust a cowboy.

At least never again.

Watching the show, she pondered the weird experience of Jed asking her out. Jed was not a remote prospect! They hadn't even gotten along that well on the judging team, for that matter. Besides, livestock guys were trouble; at the very least they were deadly to the heart. The absolute last thing that was ever going to happen to her again was to fall in love. And, if she ever did fall in love, it would most assuredly not be with a cowboy.

Since ditching her 'husband' (however regrettable the word, it was legally accurate) with Eddie's conniving help, she had several requests from local guys to go out, but she wasn't interested. Apparently, the ones who had asked were not deflected by Eddie or were brave despite his warnings that she wasn't shopping for a man. At this point she wasn't interested in a gossip-fueled local romance at all and she was grateful to Eddie for passing that message around. Someday she would be ready to flirt, and eventually date again, but not yet. It just seemed too much like giving in to someone else. Dating was in part an exercise in compromise and loss of control. Her new-found independence was in itself freeing and empowering. She wasn't going to let a man take from her again. Ever again.

Savannah watched friends and neighbors and felt like she was watching a movie of someone else's life scroll by. People were talking, people were laughing, people had relationships, kids, and jobs, whatever. She loved her farm and loved her cows. She was busy and making positive changes. But, Eddie was right about the county fair. It was the same thing, different year. County fairs were like a metaphor for life, or at least what had become her life. Suddenly, Savannah realized that while she had plenty to do, she was bored.

Maybe she did need a change of scenery.

She flipped open her phone and called Macy.

TWO

THE BOYS

As the private driver barreled up California Highway 29, Savannah and Macy were having the time of their lives. Their chauffeured ride included two bottles of chilled sparking wine, a basket of cheeses, crackers, fruit, and even glasses and little plates with "Kingsley Estate Winery and Vineyards" scrolled across the edges in gold. A handwritten note on matching cardstock read:

You must be famished from the flight-please enjoy!

— Francie

While the girls sipped and giggled in delight, Stetson, apparently oblivious to the charms of the Napa Valley, charged away on his cell, hammering at someone to 'take the deal' and it was 'a once in a lifetime package opportunity' while his booted leg tapped impatiently. Macy and Savannah flipped through the *Wine Country Today* magazines placed in the vehicle for their perusal and enjoyed Francie's treats as the car slowed and they entered the boutique town of St. Helena where Macy set to drooling at the high-end clothing shops packed together in the three-block town. Another few miles and dense woodlands appeared on ridgelines as acres upon acres of grapes stretched along the valley floor. Suddenly, they turned off the highway to meander a mile or more up a lane finally stopping at 'the cottage' as the driver called it, though it would have been considered a large old farmhouse back in the Midwest.

Outside the vehicle, the driver instantly removed their luggage and absconded with it, to where, they knew not. The air, scented with a mix of floral and musk, dusty foliage and fermentation, was heady and delicious. Something Savannah had never smelled at home also flitted on the breeze—maybe it was a mixture of sage and lavender, or just some kind of Napa Valley pixie dust, Savannah couldn't be sure. Already lulled into a pleasant state of relaxation by the beautiful drive and the sparkling wine, she took it all in with happiness; she was already infatuated with the romance and scenery of wine country.

The little party was greeted by two big labs and as they wagged tails and begged for attention, a beautiful middle-aged woman emerged from the home amid the tinkling of bangles that danced up and down her wrists as she used both arms to gush open the French patio doors and step forward onto the porch.

Crisp and dazzling in a white blouse ("Carolina Herrera, no doubt," Macy remarked, though Savannah had no idea who that designer was), Francesca Pedrocelli Kingsley was one high-class woman. Savannah immediately thought of her beautiful attorney mother, Jessica, and knew she would appreciate the elegance and alpha-woman charm that 'Francie' exuded as she demonstrated both hospitality and complete control. Savannah had always marveled at women like that. Francie's thick ash blonde hair bounced jauntily, bobbed to perfection just below her trim jawline, prompting Macy to comment once again, this time about the exceptional quality of her plastic surgery and that they'd be needing to deal with that, too, before they knew it. Savannah jabbed her in the ribs just as Francie reached the group, greeting each of them with a light hug as if they were already friends and remarking at how handsome Stetson was when he removed his hat and kissed her hand.

"It's utterly lovely here, Mrs. Kingsley," Savannah remarked, not knowing really where else to begin. "Thank you for the invitation."

Francie feigned a scowl and put an arm around Savannah's waist. "Now, I've already introduced myself as Francie, so I expect you to use my name, my dear!" she chided, then, sliding her arms around both of the girl's waists she added coyly: "Mrs. Kingsley is my mother-in-law. Or shall I say, my *late* mother-in-law, thank the Lord!"

The girls just giggled, unsure what words could be said after such a remark as Francie ushered them all inside.

"Before we get down to talking about the article, let's have some wine!" Francie exclaimed. "Boys! Come out here and greet our guests all the way from the Middle West! And – Xavier - be a pet and pour us all some of the new rose`!" she commanded while walking with flourish toward a cluster of overstuffed couches bathed in the afternoon sunlight. The view of the valley floor took Savannah's breath away as she peered through the massive bay window. She had never expected to consider grape vines beautiful, but the way the rows stretched out toward the western horizon, all as neat as an Indiana cornfield, she found utter loveliness in the scene.

"You are going to *love* the rose`! Ever had it before?" Francie began, and then answering her own question, she went on. "You do *know* its not White Zinfandel, of course. No, no! Absolutely not!" Francie exclaimed and crinkled her nose in distaste at the term. Macy observed that Francie's forehead did not move on account of regular use of Botox. She made a mental note to start getting injections the moment she returned to Oke City.

"God, those commercial-sized wineries have made such a mess of a beautiful wine with their tacky marketing ploys! Selling plunk to people of dubious taste and limited means! So totally lowbrow. After all, the French *swear* by rose` in the summer, and-" Francie paused midsentence as if right on cue, two tall twenty-something guys appeared bearing trays of salmon-colored wine and little plates of assorted cheese and crackers. Just behind them trailed the big chocolate labs sniffing everything with interest as if they'd never before been in Francie's tasting salon.

"Thank you, Dears," Francie cooed with obvious affection. "These two rogues and their mutts are my twin sons. May I present Xavier and Alexander Kingsley."

The visiting trio all reacted with a start, having expected youth or at least juveniles. Instead, 'The Boys' as Francie had called, them were two extremely handsome young men.

"Nice pair!" Macy giggled to Savannah as she smiled bewitchingly and openly admired the matched set of tall, dark-haired and hazel-eyed guys both dressed nattily in slim fitting jeans and polo shirts with popped collars. Stetson rolled his eyes slightly at his wife's silly display and stood to remove his straw cowboy hat, extending his hand.

"How ya'll doing? Thanks for having us out," he said.

"Don't hear many people say 'ya'll' around here," chuckled Brother Number One as he set down the tray, grabbed a bite of cheese, and shook hands with Stetson.

"Don't mind Xave. He's spent too much time in Europe," said Brother Number Two, the taller of the pair, Savannah noticed as she couldn't help but smile when he referred to his brother as 'Xave'. "Hi, I'm Zander," he said, addressing Savannah first. He had kind eyes and dimples on both cheeks.

"Mmmm-mmm, I bet the wine you make is delicious, Xave," drawled Macy as she continued to smile at Brother Number One. Savannah had to smirk at her and at Stetson's mild irritation.

"Actually, Zander's my wine maker," Francie piped up. "Xave's in culinary school over at the Greystone Institute."

"Yeah, with that in mind, Mother, I gotta get going. I need to check the brix on the Cabernet vineyard," Zander said turning back to the guests. "Please excuse me but I was just leaving when you arrived. Surely you will join us for dinner?"

"We'd love to!" Macy interjected again.

———————————•◆•———————————

Following an enjoyable glass of wine and a short nap at the cottage, Stetson, Macy, and Savannah found themselves awaiting dinner on Francie Kingsley's gorgeous patio. They had already talked enough about the article that Francie was totally thrilled with the idea. Explaining that her sister, Monica Pedrocelli, and Monica's husband, Hollis, ran the ranch, Francie called them and announced that she would bring the group over to the ranch in the morning.

With dinner over, Stetson set in to seriously hit Francie up on the Angus deal, leaving the girls time to chat with 'the boys'. Savannah found that she and Zander hit it off pretty well, so when he invited her on a vineyard tour the next afternoon, she was excited to accept.

They exchanged a cordial goodnight, 'The Boys' having walked them to the guesthouse across the property. "I've really enjoyed meeting you tonight, Savannah. I hope you will let me show you around tomorrow afternoon," Zander said as he stood back, but didn't make a move to leave.

"I'm so glad we got to have dinner with you and your brother, too," Savannah acknowledged. "And, yes! I really want to learn more about wine!"

Stetson and Macy exchanged worried looks; Savannah was certainly enjoying her first visit to California. But it was on the wrong side of Sonoma Mountain.

THREE
A CHAMPION-SIZED COINCIDENCE

Motivated by the beauty of the place and pleasant thoughts of Alexander 'Zander' Jefferson Kingsley's handsome face, warm hazel eyes and broad shoulders, Savannah decided an early run was the perfect way to begin her first-ever morning in the Napa Valley wine country. Thoughts of Zander's full lips, pleasant grin, and especially of his lingering hug the evening before had Savannah nearly floating down the lane toward Highway 29. But, the romantic notions had quickly faded as she huffed and puffed on her return pursuit. She had not realized what an incline that it would be and by the time she was only a quarter of the way back up, the previous evening's slight over indulgence of wine was heaving out of her pores, soaking her tank top and even the waist band of her shorts. She was drenched with sweat and was more fatigued than she had expected. She had just paused to walk –only for two minutes she assured herself - when a voice rang out from behind.

"Hey there, Pretty Lady! Watch out for the mountain lions out here!" Came the voice of Zander Kingsley as he emerged from a crop of vines and strode out on the road.

Savannah froze, not for fear of the questionable likelihood of a cougar, rather that the man she had just been thinking about was seeing her look so utterly horrible!

Zander apparently noticed her reticence to comment back. "Hey, did I spook you?" he said grinning as he advanced up the hill.

"Uh, well, not exactly," Savannah began making an effort to adjust her top and wipe away a little of the sweat. As she dabbed her face, she noticed a swath of last night's mascara came with her perspiration; she hadn't taken off her make up the evening before - a bad habit she sometimes let herself fall into-so now she was certain that her face was sweaty, red, and caked with yesterday's crusty make-up.

Zander strode up, placed his hands on his hips and smiled, waiting for her to say something.

Savannah gave into the situation; Zander's casual demeanor was catching. "Where did you come from? I never saw anybody on my way down!"

"Oh, I saw you turn around at the highway and head back up - my truck's parked on the ridge. Just checking vines along here as I do about every day this time of year," Zander began, then reaching into the zippered pocket of his Patagonia vest, he pulled out a packet of wet-wipes. "The return trip is a little more difficult than the way down." he remarked, stating the obvious.

Savannah was still embarrassed and while she accepted the wet cloth, she really just wanted to get back to the cottage and shower. "Yeah, no kidding! Not many hills like this in Indiana.

"Want a ride?"

"No, no. I am determined to finish off this hill," Savannah giggled and turned to attempt a jog again.

Zander watched her go with delight. She was about the best-looking girl he had met in quite a while. "Don't forget our tour of the wine caves this afternoon when you get back!"

"I cannot believe how different the countryside is in just the span of a few miles," remarked Savannah to Francie as they drove toward the Pedrocelli Ranch. Already the pine-lined ridges of Napa Valley had softened to more open country with sweeping vistas and rolling hills. Whereas Napa had seemed literally wall-to-wall with wineries and the corresponding traffic, once they emerged into Sonoma County, there were still pastures dotted with sheep and goats and even small dairies. The difference in the agriculture was distinct and Savannah said as much to Francie.

"Well, yes, both Sonoma and Marin County, where we are headed, are certainly more rural, or at least have a more rural feel than we do over in Napa," Francie agreed. "But, you just watch, these pastures are getting torn up by the dozens by people hungry to line their pockets with the wine industry's sprawl. It used to be entirely fruit trees, nut trees, and cattle here when Monica and I were girls, but the country is just too beautiful not to be desired by everyone, I suppose," Francie said, sounding wistful. It surprised Savannah that someone so privileged as Francie would be sentimental about land. She was in the wine business, besides!

"It is beautiful here, I love this open country, but why are people building so many wineries here?" Savannah inquired.

"It's the climate. Once you step out you'll see just how much cooler and certainly how much breezier it is. Why, you can practically see the San Pedro Bay from here, it gives on to San Francisco, so the land is just perfect for Pinot Noir and Chardonnay grapes."

Savannah listened as Francie described more about growing grapes prompting her to wonder if Francie and her husband were adding a winery in Sonoma County. "Will you be expanding your winery holdings here, too?" she asked.

"Oh God, no!" Francie exclaimed and Savannah immediately felt bad for asking, but Francie realized she had embarrassed her guest. "Oh, please excuse me for being so blunt, I didn't mean to sound rude. No, it's just that so many people are selling their ranches because they are just greedy or worse because they cannot afford to keep them. And, with development comes rules and you know, not everyone is friendly to livestock in today's world. Thank God our land is owned and is – at least right now- just far enough out west of Sonoma not to be as desirable." Francie explained.

The group drove silently for a few minutes, then Francie returned to the conversation about land. "Not that my sister and I have a lot in common - you'll see - and even though our husbands agree- and what is funny about that is they have even less in common, but anyway, our spouses both think that Monica and I *should* sell and cash in on the Pinot and Chard craze. But, we would never do it," Francie said firmly with a look that said she could not be swayed if the buyer was the King of England. As if to endorse her point even further, she added. "Our taking care of the history of this ranch and the story of our ancestors that settled the land here is important to us and we agree on the fact that preserving this ranch as a ranch is the one thing we want to do with our lives."

Savannah felt a warm kinship with Francie despite the woman's obvious advantage in financial means and culture and decided to speak up about it. "I know exactly what you mean, Francie. When I lost my dad last fall, I didn't know what to do next, but I knew for certain that keeping the farm was the one job that I needed to do."

Francie reached over and laid her hand on Savannah's, squeezing it reassuringly. She already liked the young visitor from Indiana.

———————— • ◆ • ————————

On the approach to the Pedrocelli Ranch, a massive wood and iron sign announced its presence before the car turned into the open gate. A long lane followed, lined with gnarly live oaks and tall, narrow coniferous trees Savannah surmised were some kind of pine not seen in the Midwest. The drive was board-fenced on both sides and the lane angled uphill slightly revealing olive trees, neatly planted in groomed rows and wide open meadows where Hereford and crossbred cattle appeared, attempting to graze on grass so brown that it looked more like dirt than foliage.

"Tougher country out here," Stetson commented as Macy opened her flip phone and clicked a few photos. "When is your green season, Francie?"

"Oh, winter, for certain, Dear," she commented as she lowered everyone's windows, a move that allowed a breeze scented with sage, a hint of sea air, and heady floral fragrance to fill the vehicle. "We actually have rather gloomy winters here – it's nice to see the green, but the rain makes me a little irritable. Oliver and I typically head to Palm Springs for the month of January anyway," she added, as if everyone spent a month away from home just because they didn't prefer the temperature.

Another cluster of live oaks and other trees huddled next to a sprawling ranch house designed in hacienda style. It reminded Savannah of something old Hollywood. More fragrant blooms, clearly well tended by a landscaper, filled Savannah's senses as they pulled to a stop and stepped out. Just as they did, an attractive blonde emerged from around the side of the house, clad in gardening gloves and lugging a hoe. Apparently, Savannah had been wrong about the gardener.

"Monica! I've brought your guests!" hollered Francie as she gestured for the group to approach the house. "She could have cleaned up for us!" she added in a low voice that only Savannah heard.

Monica Pedrocelli smiled pleasantly and began to remove her gloves, smoothing her long hair and tucking a piece behind one ear. She was short and thin as a reed and upon closer look, Savannah could see that she and Francie favored each other a great deal. Monica was harder looking though, perhaps because she was undoubtedly thinner, but her face bore a harsher look with a few more lines compared to Francie's smoother, 'worked on' appearance. Still the women looked great clad in tight jeans and boots and bore herself with confidence that bordered on sexy.

"I wonder how old she is?" Macy whispered.

"Shhhh!" Savannah admonished, but she was thinking the same.

"Welcome to the Pedrocelli Ranch," Monica said pleasantly and she surprised Savannah by embracing everyone lightly, including Francie who air kissed her on both cheeks. She even winked at Stetson and pinched his arm flirtatiously. "I'm so glad to meet all of you!"

The group began a cheerful exchange and Monica began to update Francie about the new barn project. "The new cowboy – as I like to call him - has done wonders, Fran, directing the layout and all. I think you'll really love it," Monica began.

"Yes, and he's using my money, too," Francie remarked as her cell phone began to jingle. "Oh! I'll pass on the showbarn tour for now. It's Lance, my decorator," Francie said as she began to step away from the group.

A dark look passed over Monica's lean, attractive face, but she quickly rearranged her expression. There was a palpable tension between the sisters, something akin to a sense of the have and have not. Savannah thought it seemed like jealousy that she sensed in Monica, though she couldn't imagine why; Monica seemed to be doing what she loved and she clearly enjoyed living at the ranch.

"My sister is hosting the Auction Napa Valley in a few months and she has already gone bonkers over starting to redecorate her house," Monica explained, turning the ignition key on a waiting Kawasaki Mule that everyone boarded. "I cannot imagine the snob factor that will be present at that event. Thank God I'll be here at the ranch!"

"You've got a gorgeous spread here, Ma'am," Stetson said, breaking the terse moment.

"Oh, Honey, don't call me, 'ma'am'! It makes me feel old – I don't seem old to you, do I?" Monica cooed as she eyed Stetson.

"No, surely not all," he muttered. It was obvious to Stetson that Monica was very pretty.

Monica left it at that and moved on. "It's really great you are here, Savannah," Monica said and began twisting her long hair into a low pony-tail. Instinctively Savannah grabbed the wheel as Monica had attempted to use her knee to steer while she fixed up her hair. Stetson and Macy were seated in the second row.

"Thanks," Monica smiled as she took over and Savannah reached inside her computer bag for her camera.

"I'm just so glad to come out, get to see the ranch and work with you personally on the article," Savannah began as she took a breath of the cool, refreshingly dry air. "You don't mind if I grab some photos while we drive around, do you?"

"Of course not! Let me tell you a bit more about the property."

They drove out of the small cluster of trees that ensconced the ranch house and passed by a small cottage. The dirt lane wound around the base of a big hill and pasture then gave on to a clearing where the new construction project was visibly under way. Monica pulled up and everyone dismounted as Savannah began snapping a few shots to test the light.

"These old traps will connect to the new the new showbarn and sale facility as this project comes together," Monica began enthusiastically. "So, I think Francie told you we both decided it was time start having production sales again-our first one in a long time is slated for this November. So, we realized the old barn just wouldn't work. Once I added a new sale cattle manager, he has really helped with getting everything to fall into place! He's working on the sale facility design and overseeing the construction, he helped decide what calves to use in the sale and which ones to leave out-" interrupting herself, she turned to Stetson and laid her hand on his chest, a move that surprised him enough that he actually stepped back. Monica was undeterred. "I cannot thank you enough, Stetson, for your recommendation of this guy we hired. Wow-he really knows what he's doing!" she added with a yet another wink.

Stetson started to squirm a bit from the unwarranted gesture, a move that set Savannah to unintended giggles. Monica turned back to her and also nodded to Macy. "Think you're smiling now, Honey, wait 'til you girls see the cowboy your friend here recommended. Holy crap he's a looker!"

"Really," Savannah smiled conspiratorially. "They must grow good looking men in California like grape vines!" She pulled her long hair up and turned back to her camera, making adjustments.

"Oh, he's not from around here at all. Stetson, where did you get this fellow from again? He was working a ranch up north, but I think he had just left some big Texas show outfit," Monica prattled on.

Savannah felt the bottom of her belly start to turn. Just as she was about to say 'Macy, what have you done?', Monica grabbed her wrist.

"Oh, Ladies, look up there! You are in for a treat!" she said, her voice absolutely dripping with saccharine. "Here comes my new man now! He's there, up on the ridge."

Savannah was looking through the lens of her camera and tilted it toward the ridgeline as Monica paused, placing a hand on her hip almost seductively. At first Savannah saw only waving grass, having zoomed in too far, but then, she recognized him. She saw his hand raking sandy brown hair flecked with sunlight blonde over one side of his face. As her camera began to take in his face at close range Savannah gasped and dropped her camera as he knees went weak…

At the same moment Stetson looked the 100 yards up the hill and recognized the tall, lithe form of his friend Cade Champion. Cade was dismounting a 4-wheeler as he approached a gate.

Cade had also looked up at that instant, recognizing Savannah. Stetson knew Cade saw only Savannah, his eyes never once leaving her face once they'd rested upon it. Cade looked stunned for a moment and his expression registered a look of surprise, then pain, and then joy. He simply stopped, leaned against the fence post and stared.

Cade Champion smiled once again at Savannah Morgan.

———————— •◆• ————————

Savannah was truly stunned into silence. She was also seething at Macy and Stetson, having grabbed Macy after she scrambled to pick herself up off the ground and fled into the half-built showbarn.

"What. Is. He. *Doing*. Here?" Savannah enunciated between breaths as she plopped roughly onto the toilet seat while Macy shut the door behind them and felt around for a light. She felt like she was going to faint or be sick or both. Her breath was coming in gasps.

"Well, turns out he's the new herdsman and sale cattle manager that the Pedrocelli Ranch hired," Macy remarked trying to sound flip. Stetson had remained outside with Monica as Macy had made Savannah's excuses, something about having to urgently use the bathroom. Fortunately, there was a restroom in the partly finished section of the building.

Savannah wasn't buying it. "You two *really* set this up? I cannot believe it!" Savannah tried to shriek but there was not enough air in her lungs to get the sound out any louder than a winded whisper. "Oh my God, I just saw Cade Champion," Savannah's head was spinning. Already little images of him were whirling around her-his eyes, his height, his mouth, his mouth on her mouth….

Macy's heart melted at the sight of her dear friend's obvious distress. She didn't know whether to laugh at her or cry with her. Truly, she and Stetson had thought there would be a more elegant way to connect their two friends, but fate had intervened before they could concoct a more perfect scenario. "It wasn't on purpose - Macy started to say, prompting Savannah's glare and incredulous look that said 'yeah right, Macy'.

"Okay, well, it wasn't at first anyway, I'll admit," Macy said leaning her rear end against the sink and sighing.

"Then how did this happen?"

"Well, here's the story. So, yes, Stetson did recommend Cade for this job when he started talking to Francie Kingsley about getting into the Angus business. You see, she mentioned that she and her sister owned a ranch and they were needing a sale cattle guy, and well, then I mentioned to Stetson that you happened to be writing an article for the breed magazine on the old Pedrocelli Ranch. Stetson had just referred Cade to her, and honestly, the coincidence was already set it motion!" Macy just shrugged and reached out to Savannah in a gesture of goodwill.

"Don't you want to talk to him at least?"

Savannah was so dizzy she had no idea what she wanted. "I can't yet," was all she could say.

She had put Cade behind her, or had at least convinced herself that she was in the process of it.

Forgetting Cade Champion now was going to be impossible.

FOUR

A WALK IN THE VINEYARD

All the way back to the Kingsley Estate Savannah kept hoping that maybe Cade would have come down off that hillside and come to her in the barn. But he didn't. Though she made Macy leave the rest room first to make sure he wasn't out there waiting on her, she had let herself hope a tiny, tiny bit that Cade *would* have been out there when she emerged, his long legs clad in tight jeans straddling the 4-wheeler while he talked with Stetson in the jocular way that men banter. What did she think – that Cade was just going to walk over to her and throw her to the ground and kiss her? That they were going to make out right there? Of course not! Hell no!

Still, when Cade hadn't been waiting to see her a heavy lump of disappointment swirled around her insides fighting with the light feathers of anticipation that were already pushing her to the brink of vomiting. When she emerged back into the bright California sunlight, the 4-wheeler was gone and Francie was there, having driven her Cadillac Escalade out to the barnlot.

"My Dear! You must have gotten too warm!" she exclaimed, fussing over Savannah and urging her back into the vehicle.

"Something like that," Macy snickered as Savannah shot her a look.

"Well, let's head back to Napa right away so you can rest a tad before dinner!"

As they drove out, Savannah leaned back, sipping the cool water Francie had provided. She looked in the rear-view mirror. She couldn't help but to do it and torture herself.

———————•◆•———————

Since it was late afternoon when they returned to the Kingsley Estate, Francie and Stetson had already agreed to drink some wine and talk cash on a buying a few Angus donor cows, leaving the girls with free time and options.

"Macy, I am guessing you are just *dying* to try the boutiques in St. Helena," Francie anticipated. "Just take the Escalade and drive back down there. There are several nice shops, of course, a few have gotten chintzy on account of the tourist hordes, but don't miss Adelle's and tell them I sent you for sure."

Macy was literally glowing with delight. Stetson groaned only slightly out of jest. Turning to Francie, he turned on his cowboy charm. "The price of those females just went up 10 percent to cover the cost of her shopping, you know that right?" he chided with a handsome grin.

"Oh, Honey, you're so midwestern. If she shops at Adelle's, you had better charge me 20 percent more to cover it!" Francie countered and she took Stetson's arm and moved him toward her office. "Meet you all here by about 8:00 to ride over to the Greystone Culinary Institute. You are going to *love* seeing Xave and his classmates. They've been prepping something phenomenal, I'm certain!"

Savannah was irritated enough at Macy that she didn't want to hear her chattering glibly about spending a small fortune at some fancy boutique so she had declined to go shopping. Alone, she strolled absently back to the pool and guest house area thinking she might sip a glass of wine or even go take another run before dinner - anything to get Cade Champion out of her brain.

But, as if on cue, a new distraction emerged.

"Hey! You're a hard one to catch!" announced Zander as he once again appeared out of nowhere and reached her side.

"Hey." Savannah smiled, pleasantly surprised.

The perfect distraction, Hot Wine Dude.

"I thought you might like that tour of the vineyards now."

"I couldn't think of anything I'd rather do," Savannah said as she flashed Zander her most gorgeous smile.

———————•◆•———————

Zander's farm truck was certainly nicer than what Savannah considered a utility vehicle at home. She actually didn't know anyone that owned a Range Rover, much less one that was used to go check fields. But, she saw the sense in it as the ridge got progressively steeper and the gravel road narrower as they drove up.

"I hope you're not too nervous about my driving," Zander jested as he took note of Savannah's white-knuckled grasp of the door handle.

His tone was playful and fun and Savannah realized she must have seemed stiff. She *had to* relax and get Cade out of her head. "Sorry, I'm just such a flat-lander, I guess!"

"Just wait 'til we get to the top-it will be worth it!" Zander said and he reached over and took Savannah's hand in his, holding it for a few minutes while he finished the ascent.

At the top of the ridge, the late summer air was noticeably cooler and Savannah was surprised that she felt suddenly chilly. "Wait here," Zander said with a smile.

She watched as he busied himself getting something from the vehicle and when he returned he brought with him a black bag and set it down on the dusty lane.

"First-we get you a little warmer," he said as he pulled a man's flannel- obviously his -from the bag and settled it over her shoulders. "It's not too smelly, I don't think," he said with a grin as Savannah accepted the wrap. "Then, we have some refreshments," he continued as he pulled two wine glasses from the bag and prompted Savannah to hold them while he pulled out a bottle and began to open it. Zander poured them each a glass and reached into the bag once again, this time for binoculars. "Third, we enjoy the view. Follow me. We walk from here!" he announced cheerily as placed the binoculars over Savannah's neck and held out his elbow for her to accept.

A short climb up the rocky path that meandered through Cabernet vines was more than enough to her get thinking about something besides Cade. The dry air was cool, yet pleasant and the wine was utterly divine. She couldn't help but realize how romantic a walk among the vineyards seemed.

"Zander, I have truly never enjoyed a wine so much," Savannah said as they settled side by side on a wide log, obviously placed there for visitors to enjoy the stunning scenery above the tree line. "This is such a wonderful time and the view is amazing!"

Zander smiled appreciatively. "I'm really glad you do like the wine. It was actually from my very first vintage as lead wine maker, the 1997. It's still young and I can taste some of the flaws, but I'm actually kinda proud of it," Zander said as he lightly swirled his glass and watched Savannah do the same, then sniff and sip again. Zander enjoyed watching her enjoy the wine. She was just so pleased to be there and so genuine. Zander didn't meet many genuine girls and certainly none as beautiful as Savannah. "I don't think I have ever enjoyed a wine as much either, but it's because of the company," he said, unable to stop smiling as his eyes lingered on her cheeks and the way the late afternoon sun was glinting off her hair. "If you're up for more fun, I have another surprise for you."

Suddenly realizing she was having a blast, Savannah drained the last sip and jumped up. "Believe me, Zander, right now I'm up for anything."

———————— • ◆ • ————————

"A mountain top vineyard tour and now the wine cave!" Savannah exclaimed as Zander pushed open the massive oak doors that gave onto the hand-built caves of Kinsley Estate Winery. "Zander! You are absolutely spoiling me!" Savannah squealed with delight and literally clapped her hands together. She knew she should feel silly and immature for being so girlish, but she just couldn't help it. It was so much fun and so uniquely different than anything to do with cows or cowboys.

"Come on in, Pretty Lady." Zander put one hand behind Savannah's back as he led her into the dimly lit cavern. Savannah's enthusiasm was catching.

A few steps in, Zander stepped over to a makeshift table where a series of lamps, candles, and large matches were displayed. "I think you'll like this," he winked as he struck one of the oversized matches and touched it to a long tray-like sconce at eye level. Just as he did, what started as one candle in the trough flickered to light and then the flame quickly spread the length of the cavern.

Savannah's eyes glowed with delight. "Zander! That is amazing!"

Zander smiled smugly, the old sconces and fire always went over well with guests. "It is cool," he acknowledged. "These old metal flame troughs were built by the original crews that dug these caves. It really was an ingenious way to have a lot of light, quickly, and safely, out of the way. When we're working in here, we go ahead and put on some of the overhead fluorescents, but for our special guests, nothing beats the ambiance."

Savannah had never seen anything like the wine cave and its series of deep, winding tunnels where row upon row of barrels lay sleeping, their heady contents aging gently amid the essence of French and American Oak. Zander carefully explained the aging process and pointed out the years each wine would await its eventual bottling and release. Finally, stopping in an area where several barrels were clearly moved down out of the racks, Zander asked if she was ready to steal a taste or two.

"Absolutely!" Savannah coed as Zander used a long glass wand, aptly called a wine thief, to extract the gorgeous garnet and violet colored samples from several barrels of Cabernet, Merlot, and Petite Verdot.

They had enjoyed quite a bit of wine when Zander paused, smiled coyly, and leaned up against a make shift bar that had been constructed to hold the sampling equipment. "Well, that concludes the tour. Anything else I can do for you this afternoon?"

Savannah knew she'd had plenty to drink and it really, really annoyed her that when Zander smiled thoughts of the roguish grin of Cade Champion came to mind.

I have to get him out of my head!

Savannah felt desperate and more than a little tipsy. Before she could stop herself, she leaned into Zander and laid a soft, silky kiss on his lips.

Zander's eyes opened wide for a moment before he found himself succumbing to the charming Savannah. He put his arm around her back and pulled her close. "Wow, and I thought Midwestern girls would be much more demure," he murmured as his lips pressed into hers. "People are fools for considering Indiana a fly over state."

———————————— • ◆ • ————————————

Savannah pounded on the door, prompting a 'Come in, ya'll' from Stetson. The little room's sliding door was open and he was sitting on the deck sipping bourbon while sharing the terms of his deal on the phone with someone back home, presumably his dad who did much of the financing for their ranch.

"Macy, I need to talk with you!" Savannah said flinging herself into the room and onto the bed.

"Sweetie, how are you doing?" Macy queried absently from the bathroom. She was fixing her already perfect hair and lipstick and modeling a new outfit. "How was the wine tour? Francie said Zander came looking for you."

"I kissed Zander."

"WHAT??"

Macy leapt out of the bathroom and onto the bed with such a force that she nearly shoved Savannah to the floor. Macy had not seen that coming. "I was only gone a couple hours and you -"

"Oh my God! WHAT? You kissed the Wine Dude?" Stetson exclaimed jumping to his feet and covering the phone receiver, his dark brows knitting with concern and surprise as he overheard the girls. "Shit! Champion is gonna freak out!"

Macy shot Stetson a look and made hand gestures to shoo him away from their conversation. "Cade is not ever going to hear about this! And, we've already been calling him '*Hot* Wine Dude', by the way."

Stetson scowled and pulled the sliding door shut as he returned to his phone call.

"Wow! That is fast moving! Really, you kissed Hot Wine Dude Number One?"

"No, No, Number Two! Zander is Hot Wine Dude Number Two! Remember, we decided that we think Hot Wine Dude Number One might be gay!" Savannah exclaimed.

Macy nodded in agreement. "Oh, yeah, that's right, we named Xave Number One and he is definitely not straight, which would make sense, why you kissed the brother. Anyway-you kissed or made out or what?"

"I know, I know. I can't believe I did it, but it was just so romantic! The view, the wine, and, well, he *was r*eally into it, too," Savannah went on.

Macy's eyes registered shock and she giggled, covering her face with her hands, an uncharacteristic move considering the amount of makeup she was likely smearing. "You just saw the man who broke your heart for the first time in eight months, then three hours later you are soliciting a kiss from a perfect stranger!"

"He's not a stranger-we met yesterday!"

"Is that *shirt* his, too?"

Savannah's hand reached up and fingered the age-worn softness of the flannel. She had actually forgotten about it. "Well, uh, it was chilly in the caves -"

Macy flipped back onto her stomach, mussing the fashionable long pixie cut, already fixing it. Suddenly, she sat straight up, eyeing her friend more closely. "You're drunk aren't you?"

Savannah shrugged and closed her eyes. "I had to do something to get Cade out of my head. The wine wasn't strong enough, I guess."

<hr />

"Are you feeling better, Dear?" Francie asked looking at Savannah who now appeared slightly drunk instead of nauseous or peeked.

"Oh, yes, I'm doing well, thank you," Savannah assured.

"I took good care of her, Mother," Zander said with a sly look in her direction. "I believe the fresh air up on the mountaintop vineyard made her feel quite a bit friskier than when you returned from the Ranch."

Savannah felt herself blush, so she took a large gulp of water and nodded along.

I cannot believe I kissed him!

"I'm so glad!" Francie remarked. "Well, Monica said that you seemed a little overcome, she was laughing because she actually thought you literally swooned over the new sale cattle manager when you saw him from afar. As if girls swoon anymore, anyway!" Francie chuckled as she waived her left wrist setting the wad of David Yurman bangles to clinking. "Of course, I probably should apologize to you, Macy, for my sister's silliness, she can be such a flirt and I'm sorry she got a bit cute with your handsome husband," Francie remarked with a disapproving look.

Macy laughed and waved it away as nothing. "That's funny, but don't worry Stetson didn't mind, did 'ya, Baby?"

"Nah, I like it when pretty ladies hit on me!" he smirked and tossed back another swig of whiskey. He was enjoying the Greystone dinner, though the portions were definitely sized for a California man and not a cowboy. He also wasn't having any wine - that was a great way to get a slamming hangover-one he was sure was well on its way for both Savannah and his wife.

"Well, I'm certainly glad she didn't offend. Her husband, Hollis - you didn't meet him today- he was around there somewhere, but anyway, he's always looking over his shoulder and worried about her fraternizing with the help. I hear the new cowboy is quite a looker - "

Savannah blanched and chocked on her wine, nearly snorting it up her nose. Macy quickly grabbed a napkin to catch the dribbles that literally leaked embarrassingly from Savannah's mouth as she mumbled something about perhaps the two of them ought to step to the restroom. Stetson tossed back another swig with a nervous chuckle at the girls. His very next thought was that he hoped to God Cade wasn't lonely enough to make a mistake with the boss lady...

Seeing Savannah's distress, Francie added, "Oh, that was tacky of me to disparage Monica that way, I shouldn't have said that!"

Savannah's mind was reeling. The 'help' Francie had so casually remarked about was *her* man....

"There are a lot of archives and files over at the ranch in the bunkhouse and in the attic and in the office. Well, honestly, there is just so much history and I'd love a project manager to go through it all and organize it into a book," Francie began not long after Macy and Savannah had returned from their rather extended bathroom trip. "I've been thinking since I met you that you would be the perfect person to organize it all. So, I want you to stay a few months and compile it all into a book!" Francie exclaimed with obvious delight at her idea.

Savannah was stunned. "Oh! I couldn't do that - I have the farm - "

Francie wasn't going to be put off." I understand, I truly do, but you must do this and it's only a short while. So, how about whatever the magazine is paying you per word for the article, I double it and voila' you have your first published book! I'll pay to have it published, of course, and Monica and I get to work on our goal of preserving the history of the ranch!"

Macy and Stetson exchanged glances. Savannah would be forced to work right on the same ranch as Cade. Their plan would come to together better than they could even imagine!

Savannah spent the better part of dessert and after dinner drinks trying to say no to Francie, but in the end, she accepted. She hoped she was saying yes for Francie and not because Cade Champion would be there everyday.

For Zander's part, he couldn't be more pleased; his mother's ability to work her magic was never something he questioned, even when he didn't ask for it. He could see what she was up to and this time he didn't mind at all. He could tell his mother absolutely adored Savannah. He knew already that he did, too.

———— •◆• ————

"I cannot believe I am actually going to do this," Savannah said breathlessly as she hugged Macy goodbye for the third time that morning. She had already called Eddie the day before and asked what the thought. His saying no or even acting the least bit resentful would have been the deciding factor. But, to her surprise, Eddie seemed sort of glad not to have her back for a while. He said he could handle it and she needed the change of scenery. Besides, with no fall shows or sales to get ready for, all he really had to do was maintain fence and handle the feeding. A year ago Savannah would have doubted him, and since she knew Eddie still had a tendency to sleep a little too late, she also consulted with Clint Cascade, who seemed equally encouraging that she stay in California for a few months. He assured her that he'd stop by every month and check on the stock.

"Give Cade another try, Savannah, please!" Macy implored.

"He's never stopped loving you, Savannah," Stetson said plainly. "I've never seen a grown man so tore up."

"Guys, I love you both, I really do. But whatever Cade and I had is over. Or, maybe it just wasn't ever there to begin with. I don't know."

Savannah wanted desperately to be mad at her meddling friends, but she wasn't, they were too sincere. But just because she wasn't exactly angry didn't mean she was running straight for Cade Champion's bed! No way would she allow herself to be swept into his web again. She was staying for the project, the fun opportunity, and maybe something interesting with Zander Kingsley.

She was not staying in California for Cade.

PART TWO

STAYING WEST

FIVE

AND SO IT BEGINS AGAIN

"Monica is expecting you this morning and she is so very, *very* excited that we're expanding the article into a written history book!" Francie exclaimed as she and Savannah breakfasted the next morning in the lovely salon. Zander's big brown lab was seated on the deck overlooking the valley as if he was watching for his master, but Zander was nowhere in sight. Savannah wondered if he regretted their kiss, but she doubted it.

"She'll be there all day to show you around the ranch and dig out all the records. I have a car for you to drive, too. Now, it's not the fanciest but the 1980's Beemer the boys learned to drive on is out front and I had the gardener gas it up for you this morning, so now you have a car to drive back and forth!" Francie added, further pleased with her set up.

Savannah felt like her life was absolutely surreal as she descended the lane and began the drive over to the ranch. Slowing as she neared a grape picking crew, she spotted Zander. He grinned from ear to ear as he approached the vehicle. Savannah couldn't help her amusement at the difference in his style compared to the type of guys she was used to being around. Zander's relaxed fitting olive green cargo trousers sported scads of zippers and he wore a Patagonia puff vest over a faded rock band tee shirt. When he placed his hand inside her window she noticed a little skull pinky ring and giggled at the thought that his fashion sense would create quite a spectacle at a cattle show.

"So, you did decide to stay!"

"Yes, your mother was more than convincing, as I am certain you well know," Savannah said with a grin.

"That's putting it mildly," Zander remarked.

"You thought I might not be here this morning?"

"Well, I wasn't sure, but I was hoping we would have much more time to get to know each other. How about dinner tonight? Maybe something much lower key than the Greystone and without my mother's meddling?"

Savannah was more than happy to accept.

<hr>

The inside of Monica's home was a complete opposite of the total couture under Francie's tutelage at Kingsley Estate. With its paneled entry way and sunken living room, Savannah assumed the old Pedrocelli ranch house was last decorated when the girls were growing up in the 1970's. Still, the home was lovely with big bay windows that enticed the eyes to gaze out at the ranch. Perhaps Monica liked the hominess of keeping the design the way it had always been, perhaps she thought it was the way it was when her parents were still there and maybe the home made her think of happier times. As she sat down at the heavy oak dining room table, Savannah wondered if she had more in common with Monica than she realized.

Any questions Savannah might have had about the state of Monica's finances compared to Francie's were quickly put to rest when Monica took a seat across from her sporting a massive diamond wedding set. With her long hair pulled back, Savannah also couldn't help but notice the (at least) one-carat diamond stud in each ear. Monica had surrounded them with boxes and stacks of papers and was beginning to explain how she had organized them when a middle aged Mexican woman placed pastries and fruit plate in front of Savannah and set down a tray laden with an ornate antique coffee urn, cups, and saucers.

"Selena, this is Savannah Morgan, the young lady I told you about that is writing a book on the ranch. She'll be in and out for a while," Monica said without looking up as Selena poured her coffee.

"Hello, Miss," Selena smiled pleasantly. "I'm very excited about the book. How do you take your coffee?"

Savannah was surprised and almost embarrassed; unlike Monica she wasn't used to someone serving her, well, anything. "Oh, my, thank you! I'll just have cream or milk - whatever you have is wonderful."

"We have whatever you want," Monica said with a flick of her wrist. "And don't worry about being so modest, its just coffee."

So the sisters are a bit more alike than I thought, Savannah mused.

The morning passed quickly as Monica laid out an oral ranch history with dizzying speed. Thankful for Selena's coffee supply, Savannah's fingers flew on her laptop as she tried to capture notes and think about a direction for the book all at the same time. The two women agreed that Savannah would sort through the boxes at her leisure, taking notes and coming to Monica at least once a week with questions or specific clarifications. Monica also promised to have a work space set up for Savannah by the next day so she would have a place to land and keep her progress organized. Savannah was excited and totally overwhelmed.

The heavy footfalls of a man in boots echoed from a back hallway mudroom giving Savannah a start. It was already midday. The moment she had been expecting had arrived. Involuntarily, Savannah licked her lips and sucked in her stomach, assuming Cade Champion would stride right into the kitchen. Instead a large barrel-chested man that looked like a middle-aged steer wrestler ambled in without saying a word and headed to the sink to wash his hands, obviously in preparation for lunch.

Hollis, no doubt, Savannah thought, judging from Francie's description of his physical traits and apparent lack of manners. On his own time, Hollis approached the table and extended a beefy hand the size of a baseball glove.

"You must be the young lady Francie hired to write the ranch history book, eh?" Hollis began as he seated himself at the table. "I'm Hollis Holmes, Monica's loving husband. Good idea about the book. A project like this might help to keep Monica out of the barn, huh, Babe?" Hollis remarked, with notable sarcasm, Savannah observed.

Monica virtually ignored him and went on where she left off. Francie had commented that Monica was a flirt, but part of Savannah could see why. Hollis didn't appear to be much of a catch from the looks of him. Between his enormous bald head and surly attitude, Savannah could see why a woman as pretty as Monica might enjoy the attention of other men.

Savannah hoped Cade was not one of them.

After a rather tense lunch where Monica and Hollis seemed to take turns jabbing each other with nasty little insults, Savannah was beginning to wish that she had said no to the book project. When he left, Monica assured her that Hollis spent all of his time but meals down at his farm shop. He liked the crops and the hay work, Monica shared, and never had been one to enjoy working with the cattle and horses like she and Francie. Savannah just hoped the three of them didn't share very many more meals.

Despite her intensity on the history with Monica, Savannah grew more anxious by the hour; she had not seen Cade and couldn't believe it. Monica hadn't even mentioned him, though that part was certainly a relief judging by the way she'd been so coy about him before. Still, every time the kitchen clock chimed the hour, Savannah assumed she'd see him. By 4:00 Monica left to run into town and told her to take off at her leisure and return tomorrow. Savannah had grown not just anxious but furious. She could not believe Cade's nerve! Over the last 8 months, he had sent her flowers, called, and yet now, here he was - on this ranch - and hadn't even come to see her! He *had to know* she was there. Savannah was pissed and when she got pissed her better judgment typically chose to run and hide. By 4:15, she had gathered her things and was seething. Instead of getting in the car to leave, she set off angrily in the direction of the show barn.

She walked, or rather stormed, up the dusty half-mile lane, not knowing what she was planning to say when she saw Cade. On approach, she craned her neck for signs of him, assuming there would be a truck or a 4-wheeler, something to indicate that Cade was working in the new barn. But she didn't see a vehicle parked anywhere. Curious just the same, Savannah stepped into partially constructed building and began snooping around, her irritation growing by the minute as she mumbled her herself about what an ass Cade Champion really, really, *really* was anyway.

Then, just like that, Savannah felt a presence. A warmth and tingling came over her like a veil and her arm hair rose. Savannah whirled around.

Cade Champion was there.

He leaned against one of the new white stall gates, just watching her as if he'd been there all along, maybe he had. His tall, long-legged form was cast against the hazy light of the late afternoon sun giving his dark blonde hair a golden hue. His easy grin and hopeful eyes took her breath away. She felt herself stagger as she involuntarily whispered: "Cade."

"Savannah Pence Morgan. I've been waiting to see you all day."

A white-hot core of pure emotion fluttered through Savannah. She wanted to be mad, or something, *anything,* but she was just all jitters.

Cade approached her, covering the distance in three long strides. His eyes were glowing, Savannah was almost certain she saw tears at the corners, as he held out his arms. "My God, you're so beautiful. I, I, have missed you," he breathed as he pulled her to him. Savannah started to melt, started to feel the downward swirling that always happened when Cade was near. His hands were in her hair. He was whispering something. "I was hoping you would come to me, I've missed you so much, I cannot believe you are here - "

That snapped Savannah back into the present and her present state of mind, she reminded herself, was angry! She flung herself back with such force she lost balance and skidded across the dirt floor on her butt. Cade lurched forward to help her up, but she shoved herself backward from his reach, kicking with her feet in a backwards crab move. The tears came now, flooding her eyes, dampening the dust on her cheeks that she had kicked up. "That's - that's - just bullshit, Cade! You weren't waiting on me! I've been here all damn day!" she cried.

Cade looked chastised then frustrated. He certainly hadn't forgotten her temper.

"Savannah, I just learned you were here from Hollis about an hour ago. I drove right over here from the south ranch as soon as I heard," Cade's voice softened. "I cannot believe you are going to be here to write a book. We have another chance -"

"Don't even think about it!" Savannah tried to sneer at him, but more tears came, mangling the words. She backed up again, attempting to wipe her eyes with one hand, a move that created a smear of mud across her cheek.

Cade felt physical pain at the sight of Savannah crying. He still loved her.

"Savannah, please, let me help you up," he knelt in front of her, his left hand lightly touching her knee, while his long lean fingers closed gently around Savannah's right shoulder, beginning to lift her.

"I'm sorry, am I interrupting something?" came Monica's voice. She stood in the doorway, now clad in a snug low-cut tank top and her typical tight jeans. She held two long neck beers.

Savannah stumbled back from Cade. "I-uh- was just thinking of heading back to Kingsley's, Monica," she grunted and pulled herself to her feet, attempting the wipe away the dust. "Thank you for the hospitality, I'm really going to enjoy this project. Excuse me," Savannah said weakly and fled from the area, her eyes red with tears.

This time Cade let her go, turning to smack his palm sharply against the wall.

A tight knot of jealousy pooled in the pit of Monica's belly as she smirked and watched the girl go. Cade did not like the catty expression she wore when he turned back to face her. "You two have a history I see."

"Is it that obvious?" Cade asked, sitting down on a bale of hay and feathering his hair. The collar of his shirt was open and his dark blonde chest hair glistened with sweat. Monica moistened her lips as she looked at him.

This one is the sexiest one we've hired yet, she thought hungrily.

Monica had brought out only two beers since she hadn't expected company. She opened the top of one and handed it to Cade. He grimaced and accepted it, but instead of staying to talk he muttered 'excuse me' and strode out of the barn. Monica watched the fine, firm shape of his backside as he clamored onto the 4-wheeler and gunned it out to the pasture. She had been bringing Cade a beer around chore time for the better part of two weeks, and while he always stayed to drink it with her, he had always kept the conversation specific to the show barn and the sale. Despite her hints, Monica finally figured out why her sexy fish wasn't biting.

———————— • ◆ • ————————

Savannah arrived at the ranch the next day completely confused about what to do. When she left the evening before, she just drove and ended up canceling dinner with Zander. She was crying and felt too weak to bother being seen. Zander seemed disappointed but didn't push her for reasons, but he had already stopped by the cottage this morning to see how she was feeling and reschedule. Though the dawn of a new day had her seeing more clearly, she couldn't help but think that she might be headed for trouble by being in California and working on the same ranch as Cade.

She entered the mudroom without knocking as Monica had instructed her to do and was met by Selena who showed her to a little alcove off the hallway where she was outfitted with a desk and leather covered chair. Despite the formidable stack of boxes and papers to sift through, it was a cheerful set up with a big window that faced west looking out at one of the main pastures. Savannah felt satisfied that she could work comfortably there as long as Cade was nowhere in sight. As she settled in, Selena returned with coffee and a few pastries pausing to let her know that Monica wouldn't be around for the day. "She also left word that you might want to head over to the cottage and start digging out some of the archives in there," Selena relayed. "Let me tell you, that storage room in there is stuffed with artifacts, so you'll be looking in there for a while!"

Savannah spent the morning at her new desk categorizing the papers with sticky notes in an effort to create a systematized way to read through everything. She was grateful when Selena came to her around noon inquiring about lunch. Savannah started to hesitate, with Monica gone she didn't really want to eat lunch alone with the churlish Hollis, but Selena, sensing her tension, assured her that wouldn't be the case. "Hollis isn't here today either, Miss. He and the New Cowboy are up gathering some calves at a ranch about two hours from here."

Feeling her shoulders shrug in relief, she eagerly stood to follow Selena to the kitchen. "Oh that's interesting. Monica mentioned that Hollis doesn't much like the cattle work."

Selena nodded as she ladled out a bowl of tortilla soup for Savannah. "Mmn-hmm, that's true, he doesn't much like cows. But the ranch is short of help right now with getting ready for the new sale and I overhead him say they had to weld some pipe gates. That's the kind of work he does."

Having returned to her quarters after lunch, by 3:00 Savannah was beginning to feel cagey and decided she would investigate the cottage storage room.

A short walk from the main ranch house, the cottage was a darling little two-story house set back slightly off the lane. The front was well tended with fresh landscaping and planter boxes adorned the windows of the porch. Savannah knocked as she approached because it was suddenly apparent that it was a guesthouse and she hadn't thought to ask if someone was staying there. But, hearing no one and with free reign given by Monica, she stepped inside. Entering the tidy little kitchen the smell of a man's home was permeating. Savannah instantly realized the cottage did in fact have a guest - Cade. The smell of his cologne hung muskily in the breezy air of the space making Savannah's knees weaken momentarily.

Maybe I shouldn't be here, she whispered aloud.

Savannah froze with indecision. Maybe she shouldn't come into the cottage and be near Cade's things or maybe she should just ask Monica to have the storage room cleaned out and all its contents sent to the ranch house. But yet as Savannah glanced around, curiosity began to pervade her senses; maybe she *did* want to know what was in the cottage. She stood, taking it in for a moment, the late afternoon sun seeping into the windows, illuminating all the trappings of Cade and the life she didn't know about him. There were so many things she didn't know; they'd had so little time together.

He was neat, she noticed, by the way only a couple dishes were stacked, rinsed, in the sink and the way he left his clean cowboy boots by the back door. There were all these little signs of him, things she had never touched: A pair of faded white cotton gloves, leather jacket on the back of a chair, a blue *King Ropes* ball cap hanging by the door. Stepping into the living room, she noticed breed magazines scattered at the foot of a dilapidated easy chair, a glass of whiskey with just one sip left on the side table along with a plastic container of pretzel rods. These were the little things about how Cade lived, how he had been living in the eight months since she had seen him, and how he lived in the 35 years before they met. Savannah closed her eyes and sighed. These were all the little things about being a part of his life that she would only know if she shared his space, his life, his bed…

A warm, strong arm was suddenly, but gently, around her waist…

"Savannah."

Cade was there, slipping in behind her turning her head and kissing her….

Savannah started to stiffen from surprise.

How does a man his size sneak up so easily!

But the arms were strong, the scent of Cade so familiar and exciting, his lips so damn delicious.

"Savannah," Cade murmured. "Savannah, you've come to me," he whispered.

Cade kissed her and she kissed him back fiercely, melting into the sensual delight of it.

"Say you love me, let me love you still," Cade breathed.

"No!" Savannah pulled herself back to reality. "No! I will not do this!" she exclaimed. "Cade, you can't – we can't just start over like nothing happened!" she cried out, her eyes flooding with tears.

Savannah was ready to be defensive, but instead of pushing her, Cade gently stepped back and sighed. "You're right, Savannah, we can't pretend we didn't part ways and hurt each other. But please don't run off today. Come on, let's talk - at least look at me," Cade added, the start of his stunning grin curving around his mouth.

Cade stepped to the fridge and grabbed two beers. "Let's go sit down outside."

Savannah hesitated a moment. Being with Cade Champion was dangerous, lethal in fact, to her plans to stay single and independent, but Savannah *wanted* to stay. As she watched him pull two Adirondack chairs around on the cottage's porch, she felt an over whelming desire just to look at him. The way his jeans cupped his thighs and his broad shoulders strained against the worn cotton button-down shirt were enough to get her started on some very bad thoughts that she had strictly forbidden herself to remember, but…

Cade caught her watching him and he smiled slowly, easily, as his lean, muscular forearm held out a long neck, beckoning her to sit down.

What was the harm with just one beer…

———————— • ◆ • ————————

Savannah and Cade sipped silently for a few moments, neither knowing what to say or where to begin. Finally, Cade turned to her and in the way she remembered that he did, he just looked at her. Savannah held his gaze for a moment, searching his eyes from across the safe distance of a few feet. She felt his gaze boldly exploring the contours of her face, her neck, and lower. Time was suddenly slow, she felt herself shudder, perhaps it was from the icy condensation of the beer as it dripped onto her wrists or maybe it was from the way she felt at meeting Cade's eyes once again. Finally, he broke off his perusal of her and puffed out a big breath. While leaning back in his chair, he took a long drink, and feathered back his hair.

"So, Hi."

"Hi."

"Where do we start?" Cade asked, his expression looking pained again, more serious suddenly.

Savannah felt herself relax a little as she looked out at the picturesque horizon.

I'm in beautiful California wine country, sitting on a porch drinking beer with the man I swore I would never speak to again, Savannah thought. *Life is full of surprises.*

"Cade, I don't know. The way we left it, I -"

Cade's hand came up, palm open as if in admission. "It's my fault, I handled Denver badly. I screwed up. I know that. But, I had just fallen so hard for you and when I found out you were married and didn't tell me, Savannah," his voice trailed off.

Savannah could see his hurt, but she didn't want to. She wanted to be mad at him, to believe that he was the only one that did the wrong and that she didn't want or need him back.

"Cade, I am sorry, but you didn't give me a chance."

"I know I didn't. Hey, let's not go into all this right now," he remarked, perking up a bit. "It's been months since I've seen you and you look beautiful."

"Thank you."

"How about we just start slow, can you do that?"

Savannah shook her head no. She had to keep her wits with him. "Cade, I don't know where we go from here," Savannah said heavily.

"Judging from that kiss you laid on me, I have a idea…"

"Cade!" Savannah blushed rapidly. She couldn't believe the way she'd responded when he touched her. He blew her mind the way he really did drive her wild. "I don't think so!"

Cade chuckled. "Okay, I won't push you. What if we start tomorrow with a ranch tour?"

Then, as if she had already answered yes, he stood and stepped back into the kitchen. Savannah shook her head when Cade returned to offer her another beer but she ended up accepting it anyway.

It was well after dark when Savannah stepped off the porch and floated to the car. They had talked for hours about everything carefully avoiding the subject of 'them'. She caught him up on her cowherd program, on the deal she cut with Eddie, and about Clint Cascade buying half of Tiara. He told her about the ranch in Montana, the shearing crew, and how Stetson called him about the job in California. It had been easy, it had been fun; it had been as though Cade had always been in her life.

She told herself she would be cool, she could handle it, she could just be near Cade and be fine. But, she was not going to be in a relationship with him again.

Cade watched her leave as he leaned against the porch's columned spindle, one long booted leg on the top step the other on the railing.

"I'm a patient man, Savannah," Cade called out to her as she started the car. "I told you that before."

Savannah shook her head, as if to say 'no' to him once again, but he thought he caught the hint of a smile.

He was going to enjoy falling back in love with Savannah. As he grabbed another beer, he knew he had never fallen out.

———————— • ◆ • ————————

On her third morning at the Pedrocelli Ranch, Savannah arrived completely conflicted and exhausted. She had probably slept a total of ten minutes the previous night. Her mind, or was it her heart, overruling her desire to sleep as it recounted every second of the evening with Cade on the porch.

When she pulled into Monica's driveway she was wired and anxious. She had decided that if Cade did come looking for her about the ranch tour (and maybe he would forget) that she would simply say no and go straight back to working on the book. But as she pulled up to the house, her best-laid plans, as they always seemed to be where Cade Champion was concerned, were pushed aside. Cade was there, leaning against his truck as if he had nothing better to do, his long legs crossed at the ankles. He was sipping from a big Styrofoam convenience store cup. Another sat on the hood of the pick up.

"I was afraid you might try to bail on our tour, so I thought I'd be ready," Cade said with a charming grin as he handed the drink to her. "I got you an iced tea from Gino's Café - you'll love it, they make delicious iced tea over there."

Savannah could practically smell the clean, freshly showered scent of Cade's skin from where she stood. When she accepted the drink, his fingers lingered on hers just a beat too long. Memories of being in bed against that clean, warm chest fluttered up in her like a wave.

Get a hold of yourself!

Cade grinned as if he could read her thoughts. "Damn, you look awesome today," he said admiringly. "Ready?"

"Not without me!" came Monica's voice. She emerged from around the side of the house, gardening gloves on. "Cade, where are you two headed?"

Savannah felt herself groan inwardly. Monica, her shirt unbuttoned one too many, was *not* who Savannah had wanted Cade to see this morning.

"Hey, uh, there, Monica. I thought I'd give Savannah a ranch tour so she could get some photos for her book project."

"That's an excellent idea, Cade," she chirped. "I'm ready!"

Cade started to say something but Savannah shot him a look so that he wouldn't. Monica acted as though she didn't notice and had already headed for the front passenger seat of Cade's pick up, grabbing up the iced tea off the hood as she slid in. "Oh Cade, thank you! I just love Gino's iced tea."

———————— •◆• ————————

As it turned out, having Monica along for the morning tour was just fine and accomplished two objectives. First, Savannah didn't have to be alone with Cade most of the day in a truck, something that could have easily led to more, knowing him. Two, with the distraction of a third party, Savannah was actually able to concentrate on taking pictures, listening to Monica describe the ranch and ask formative questions for her notes. If she had been alone with Cade, she probably would have forgotten her brain, as good as he looked every time she let herself catch a sideways glance at him. Despite Monica's presence, he had boldly winked at her in the rear view mirror twice. She had to giggle at the memory of what those winks had caused her to do back in Denver.

Considering Monica, Savannah realized that was the third good reason to have her along - to keep the older woman right where she could see her. Monica was obviously no saint and Savannah wouldn't be surprised if what Francie had said about her 'fraternizing with the help' was true. Every occasion she got, Monica bent forward a little too far revealing her breasts in the just-a-little-too-low-cut blouse. Or, if they hit a bump in the pasture she managed to slump into Cade on the front seat bench and stay a bit too long. Finally, as she was directing Cade to take a turn and drive up to an old homestead site, she even laid her left hand on his thigh – and *left it there* - way too long for Savannah's taste.

For his part, Cade didn't appear to taking the bait – and whatever else - Monica was so obviously offering. But Savannah couldn't help but wonder if he had, or if he would if she continued to reject him. Savannah's thoughts were a jumbled mess! She didn't want Cade, didn't want his transient cowboy lifestyle, didn't like the way her feelings for him seemed to give him control over her, and she hadn't yet decided to give up on being mad about how he had left Denver. Still, the thought of him and Monica made her ill.

She would be keeping her eyes on Monica, that was for certain.

After she lunched with Monica and Hollis, she spent the afternoon working back at the ranch. Near 4:00, her cell phone rang with a California number.

"Hey, there is one part of the tour you didn't get to see this morning."

"Cade?"

"Yep, got a new cell phone since I am sure you must have blocked my number from the last one," he quipped.

She had. "Well, I -"

"Forget about it and DON'T lose this one. Come out to the new barn. A bunch of things got installed the last couple a days and I want to show it to you."

Cade was running a drill gun as Savannah ducked into the new barn escaping the brash sunlight of the California afternoon. He didn't hear her approach and was hoisting a brand new white metal gate, its high gloss paint gleaming almost blue-lavender, balancing it on his knee while he had the extra drill bits in his mouth. The muscles of his thighs strained to steady the gate while holding the drill against the wall brace. Savannah rushed to help him, bending down to hoist up the gate in support.

"Hmm!" Cade mouthed a greeting and nodded. Savannah smiled, noticing the little beads of sweat on his temples and the musky scent of his skin. On impulse she reached up and gently withdrew the two drill bits from his lips. Cade paused long enough in his efforts to give her a coy eyebrow raise as he licked his lips almost seductively.

"Hey, thank you," he said and winked.

Savannah started to blush in spite of herself and turned away. "Don't get any ideas, its just dangerous to have something like that in your mouth."

"Do you have a better idea of what I could put in there?"

As soon as she'd made the mouth remark, she should have known Cade would take it south.

Typical!

Cade chucked at her apparent embarrassment. "Okay, help me lift this thing when I tell you to. I think I've about got it to hang right," he said and giving the word, the new gate attached, bobbing jauntily a moment against the hinges. "Not bad, but I wish I didn't have 30 more to go," Cade grimaced as he nodded toward two enormous stacks of gates wrapped in plastic. "Glad you're here, it's a good time for a break!"

Savannah was surprised that someone who was supposed to be a show cattle manager would be doing the manual labor and said as much.

"I dunno, I guess I just like to do the work myself."

"Well, it seems like Francie and Monica have plenty of money to hire somebody to come in and do it," Savannah quipped.

Cade shrugged. "I 'spose they do, but I told Mon that I'd like to supervise and do some of the work myself. You can't trust a towny contractor to know how the hell a showbarn ought to be set up, ya know?"

Savannah's nose involuntarily flickered at the sound of Cade using the nickname 'Mon' for Monica.

How close are they?

"Anyway, I'm really grateful to the ladies for letting me set up the barn myself. I've worked out of a lot of barns, but in all my road days, I've never built a barn from scratch," he said, indicating for her to follow him.

"Looks to me like you're having fun," Savannah remarked as Cade demonstrated the network of pens and alleyways.

"You could say that," he said wistfully, then turning to her he added, "Especially now that I get to see your beautiful face everyday."

"Cade, come on, just show me the set up."

"Okay, okay," he laughed, holding his hands up as if he couldn't help himself. Savannah felt her insides get gushy.

Cade was so good-looking sometimes it just made her ache.

As walked the length of the new build, it was obvious he had done a lot in just a few day's time. Cade explained the flow from the unloading area where a 'hot box' would be set up to catch cattle that weren't broke or be used to load them onto a trailer. He showed her the alley where they would lead in new cattle from the various traps outside that were being built to accommodate heifers on feed during the season. He demonstrated the wash rack, its fresh concrete smooth and cool, and then the clipping area and finally even a cooler room he was constructing. Pallets of fresh shavings had been delivered to bed the stalls and the automatic waterers, one shared by every two stalls, had been set. Cade had special brackets created to hang blowers and cords out of the way and rows of brand new Sullivan's Turbo fans were stacked ready for install, two for each pen.

"There's where I didn't spare the expense," he said indicating the fans and the brand new blowers. I'd rather have all the equipment and want and save money on the labor."

"It looks like you've thought of everything. This showbarn is really awesome!" Savannah was impressed. She thought of her own wooden barn at home and the definite upgrade that it needed. Cade's perfectly planned barn at the Pedrocelli Ranch was definitely a thing of cowboy envy.

"Well, you haven't seen one of the best parts yet!" he said as he opened the big doors that gave on to the new sale facility. Entering from the barn, guests could easily come into a large hospitality area equipped with a kitchen, areas for table seating, offices, and space for a bar. "Bar isn't quite stocked yet, but we do have a fridge! Ready for one?" Cade inquired as he leaned in and grabbed them both a Coors Light. "This area is definitely going to be Francie's domain. She is already talking about how there isn't enough room in here for the sale party she is planning to throw, so I guess she is renting a big fancy tent that will be set up on the other side of these doors, too. Now, let me show the rest," he said sweeping his hand out gesturing through a gapping hole that was an unfinished entryway. It opened to the sale ring and bleachers.

"There is *a lot* left to do in here, but picture it with me," Cade seemed to breathe into her ear. He stood behind her, delicately placing a hand on her left shoulder while the other pointed over her right indicating his vision.

"There's where the sale ring and auction block will set and how the chutes would come in from the back one direction and out the other as each cow goes through the ring. The auction block will have this kinda cool raised area for special guests or family - another of Francie's ideas," Cade shrugged. "I don't know who she thinks will be coming that will need that fancy seating, but you know her," he laughed, not unkindly. Savannah scanned the entire room, noticing it was at least two stories high and lined with windows for natural light. A staircase led up to what looked like an apartment of office.

"What's up there?"

"It's gonna be an apartment and a manager's office. If I were staying, I'd move out here, but I'm not, so -"

"Why not? Stay, I mean?"

Cade turned her to face him, his cobalt blue eyes round and thickly rimmed with his dark lashes. He started a smile. "I was hoping I'd have other plans besides California, Savannah."

Savannah met his gaze. "If I had set up a cool facility like this and had money to play with in the show cattle business, I'd want to stay and have more sales a year."

Cade laughed lightly. There was something so innocent about her. "It's not as simple as all this, Savannah. Look, I love working sales, but eventually you have to answer for whatever you do for an owner, no matter how much jack they've got. I got a buddy, he's the high flying auctioneer, Woody Valentine, that says you might as well take your money – he says take about two-thirds of it - and put it the middle of this fancy sale ring and light it on fire and then go get some hotdogs and beer and make a roast out of it cause when you put on a big deal sale like this you gotta be rich or stupid."

Savannah laughed aloud. "All this not to make any money?"

"Oh you bring in money on sales - I've run million dollar sales before for big-deal guys. But, in the end, do they net a damn thing? Who knows! If you ask Valentine, he'd say sometimes they don't."

"Well, he and you get paid all the same though, right," Savannah giggled, flirting a little with Cade as she lightly flicked her hand against his arm, pretending to show disdain.

"Damn straight! I'm way too old to work cows for free!"

Savannah smiled again. They were having a great time; they were talking, really talking. She found her stomach fluttering up and down.

Be careful, be careful.

Cade leaned closer, his joking smirk turning more serious, his eyes getting that sexy quality again when the crinkles around the corners softened. "Actually, the real reason I'm not planning on staying is that I'd love to come to Indiana and set up a barn like this for you if you like it so well, Savannah," Cade said without a hint of teasing in his voice. He was dead serious.

Savannah was completely startled, but saved from answering by the ring of her cell phone. She pulled it from the bejeweled holster on her belt loop.

Shit! Zander! I forgot about our date!

Savannah stepped away to speak with him knowing he was calling because she was already late to meet him.

I cannot believe I completely lost track of time! Savannah thought as she returned to Cade's side.

"Who was that?" Cade inquired, as if to whom she spoke was automatically his business.

"It was, uh, the Kingsley's, actually."

"Oh yeah? You having dinner with Francie tonight?" Cade had obviously overheard her confirming plans. "I bet that's fancy," he said, attempting a little joke. "You met the rest of her family yet? Monica said she has a couple nephews that are a little on the feminine side," Cade said, smirking.

Zander Kingsely and whether or not he was 'a little feminine' was the absolute *last thing* Savannah wanted to discuss with Cade. Thoughts of she and Macy's 'Hot Wine Dude' nicknames fluttered across her mind.

Savannah found herself making excuses about how she needed to leave because she was going to late for the dinner reservations - which was true since it was already past the time she had told Zander she would meet him.

"Sure, well, have fun tonight. Francie is quite the classy lady. I'm sure you like her," Cade remarked. She waved away his offer to drive her back to her car on the mule, feeling an overwhelming need to get away from him – and the guilt she was already feeling.

Savannah could not believe it. She was already lying to Cade about 'the other man'.

Again.

If she didn't want Cade, then why she didn't admit to him that she had a date with Zander?

SIX

A PICNIC IN THE VINEYARD

S avannah felt restless when she returned from going out with Zander. They'd had fun, but she needed to be alone. When he invited her to come to his place, she deferred 'until next time' and cut their date a little short.

She started to think about the farm, so pouring herself a glass of wine, she called Eddie.

"You do realize its after midnight in Indiana, right?" Eddie said, grouchily.

"Sorry, Eddie," Savannah hadn't considered the time or that Eddie would care. He was kind of a night owl. "But I just got back from going out and I had been thinking about those embryos we got on Tiara and how we need to get those put in soon so we can have fall calves next year. So, I thought you'd want to talk about it now -"

"It's not exactly a good time, Savvy - uh, why don't I call you tomorrow, okay?" Eddie grumbled. Just as Savannah was started to affirm that tomorrow would be fine, she heard feminine sounds in the background.

"Edd-eee, hon-eee, come back to bed, bay-bee," mewed a female voice on Eddie's line.

"Hey, like I said, I really gotta go. Call ya tomorrow," Eddie said sharply as he hung up.

Savannah laughed out loud. *Eddie had a girl!* Her first thought was how much fun it would be to tell Cade.

Cade.

Why is it always Cade?

———————————— • ◆ • ————————————

The next morning she called Monica and let her know that she wouldn't be coming over for a few days. Savannah had been up half the night when she finally decided just to get up at 5:00; her restlessness was definitely due to Cade. A few days away from the ranch would help, she assured herself. Besides, she was anxious to start actually crafting something out of the research she had been accumulating.

By noon she had enjoyed a nice run and talked to Eddie and Clint about the farm and the need to get embryos put in on the Tiara cow. She was starting to feel guilty about being gone, but Eddie assured her that he had things under control. He was actually chipper, too – probably due to the nocturnal guest he'd had the night before, Savannah giggled to herself.

Francie had offered a standing invitation to come and enjoy lunch with her at noon, so she fixed her hair, added some mascara and lip gloss and decided that lunch with Francie and a book update talk would be fun.

"I'm delighted you're going to be here a couple of days working, Dear," Francie remarked as she placed a bejeweled hand on Savannah's wrist. Her 'light lunch' was incredible complete with crab cakes, steamed asparagus, and, of course, rose`.

"I'll enjoy having you around," Francie commented as she took a delicate bite.

"I'm looking forward to digging in a little on the research and starting to put together an outline to show you," Savannah said, sipping rose`. She couldn't have too much or she'd be napping all afternoon.

"Yes, I assume you've dug up quite a bit, with as much as you've been at the ranch. Zander says you've been putting in rather long hours over there."

Savannah felt herself blush at the thought of why and she put her napkin to her mouth as a diversion. "Ah, yes, there is a lot to look at."

"Savannah, you've mentioned your mother a few times, I wondered if you might like to invite her out sometime soon. We could all rent a limo and do some tasting. What do you think of that?"

Savannah was shocked by the generosity of yet another invite. Jessica would love it, she was certain. It would be good to be with her mom, too.

"That's a wonderful offer, Francie! I'll call her today!"

"I cannot wait to meet her, she must be lovely."

"Hey! I was hoping you'd be here!" Zander said in a rush as he bounded into the room, pausing to kiss his mother on the cheek. He sat down across from Savannah and poured himself a short glass of rose`.

"Have some lunch with us, Alexander," Francie suggested.

"Nope, can't Mother. I'm moving a new crew this afternoon, but we'll be done by 4:00 if I push them," he said and taking a sip he turned to Savannah, smiling almost sheepishly. "I came here to offer you a little surprise," he began. Savannah arched her brows prettily at the mention of a surprise in front of Francie.

"Yep, since I know I'm really busy with harvest and you're staying late at the ranch a lot, I thought I should try and show you a better time. Xave has helped me concoct a nice little picnic for us this evening. Will you go with me?" he said, his handsome face open and hopeful.

"I'd love to! When are we going?"

"Meet me at 5:00 at the stables. Bring a sweater, we're going to ride up the to the hilltop and have dinner in the vineyards," Zander announced, almost giddily.

"You have a stables here?" Savannah inquired.

Macy was going to be impressed by this story!

Savannah in fact did call Macy to inquire about what a girl wears when riding a horse, with a handsome man, to attend an evening dinner in the vineyards. She wanted to look sexy, but needed to be warm, too. Savannah had Macy on speakerphone as she curled her hair and put on makeup. Because she hadn't packed for more than a week, she didn't have a lot to choose from. Francie had already offered to ship some of Savannah's clothes out, but Savannah had no idea who would pack them for her-certainly not Eddie!

"Who cares what you're wearing! Play up your assets, Baby! You've got boobs, use 'em!" were Macy's typical suggestions.

Pondering those, Savannah selected jeans and boots, but with a low cut top she could put a jacket and scarf over when she wasn't displaying her 'assets' seductively. She was finishing her make-up when her cell rang.

It was Cade.

"Hey."

"Hey."

"Just checking to make sure you've kept my new cell phone number!" Cade remarked, teasing her about her months of unreturned phone calls.

"I'll see what I can do to lock it in my contacts this time," Savannah said with a smile in her voice. "In case I need something at the ranch with regard to the book and all."

"Yeah, of course," Cade quipped. "I was planning to talk with you about this the next time you were at the ranch, but you didn't tell me you were going on a hiatus."

Savannah bristled and yet felt a little flutter in her stomach.

Had Cade missed her the last few days?

"Well, I've been doing some writing."

"Oh, that's good. Well, anyway, I got to thinking you would probably be missing cows about now and well, my crew help is not that great. Any chance you'd be willing to come over and help me out working cows this weekend?"

Cade's request caught Savannah by surprise. "Oh, I, uh, well, I don't know about that."

"Hollis is going to help out, too, so we'd be supervised, if that is what you are worried about."

Savannah laughed in spite of herself. "I tell you what, Cade Champion, I'll think about it."

She flipped her phone shut and checked her hair once again. She thought about putting it in her purse, but decided against it. If they were going to the vineyard, she would 't have reception and besides, she didn't want to think about Cade Champion tonight.

———————— • ◆ • ————————

In Indiana, people would have referred to it as a barn rather than a 'stables', the word 'stable' sounding pretentious, but everything about Zander's 'Napa Valley Cool' lifestyle was more elevated than anything Savannah had ever experienced. The 12-stall facility was spotless and shaded by a gathering of old live oaks. The smell of eucalyptus hung in the warm early evening air that blew down off the sage-colored hills. Zander and a groom were readying the mounts as Savannah approached, her apprehension building. She'd only seldom ridden horses.

"Savannah! Hey, ready to ride?" Zander asked as he adjusted the girth. Savannah laughed silently to herself about the fact that she stressed about her outfit. Zander wore the funniest clothes; he sported a pair of slim fitting stretch jeans that were tucked into equestrian boots, a mock turtleneck and a beret.

Savannah smiled sheepishly as she reached up to stroke the horse's neck. "I'm ready, but I have to admit, I have only ridden horses a handful of times in my life."

"Well, that's perfect because you've come to the right place for help. I happen to be an equestrian champion and have been riding my entire life!" Zander bragged. To Savannah's surprise he leapt onto his horse, stirred the mount around sending him running and then jumped him over a set of low fences!

Savannah clasped her hands to her mouth in delight and shock. "Oh my Gosh, Zander! Way to make me feel like an idiot!"

Zander trotted his horse over to her, reaching down to grab her arm and as he did, he leaned in to give her a short, sexy kiss on the lips. "Not possible - you look too hot to be anything but awesome."

Savannah felt the edges of her fingertips tingle.

Not so effeminate after all, huh, Cade?

———————— ◆ ————————

"So, these are the highest Cabernet vineyards in the entire Napa Valley," Zander was saying as they weaved slowly along the hilly dirt path.

"So, how soon do you harvest these?" Savannah asked, they had been riding for about 20 minutes and her heart was finally settling down. Zander had stayed close to her and guided her up the hillsides, picking the route. He was amazingly comfortable on horseback.

"Well, technically the higher the elevation, the later the harvest. But it's also about the age of the vineyard, the slope of the hillside and the weather conditions," Zander explained. "Hey! Here comes your surprise!" he announced as he kicked his horse into a trot.

Just up ahead, past the end of the row of vines was the most gourmet site she'd ever witnessed. A wooden table was set with a beautiful display of food and wines; it was laden with fancy cheeses, crackers, antipasto, breads, decadent looking little tarts, and fruit. There were multiple bottles of wine already opened and covered platters that presumably held more delicacies. An assortment of tall candles and beautiful flowers decorated the table and flaming torches created a boundary around the clearing. A canopy hung overhead, making the area seem like a room with a vineyard view.

Zander was already dismounting, his eyes glowing with delight at the set up.

"Zander!" Savannah gushed. "I couldn't have imagined anything more perfect in my wildest dreams!"

"Well, I felt like I wasn't making much of an impression on you, so I thought maybe I'd up my game," Zander remarked, extending his hand to help her down.

"And! He of course needed the *talented* help of his favorite little foodie fairy!" announced Xave as he emerged from the vines. "Do you like?"

Savannah launched into giggles at Xave's reference to himself as a 'food fairy'. "I wondered who set this all up! It's amazing, Xave!"

"Yeah, I know," he said fluttering his hands. "Well, Bro, it's up to you now buddy," he leaned in and kissed Savannah on the check, then he feigned a frown. "You're so pretty! But yep, still gay!" he laughed flamboyantly then hustled over to his waiting 4-wheeler and careened down into the vines.

"You ate nearly every single bite of cheese!" Zander teased Savannah as he later poured her another glass of Cabernet. "I have never seen a girl eat cheese like that before!" he laughed again.

Savannah probably should have been embarrassed – she had eaten a lot of the delicious cheese board replete with brie, blue, parmesans, and some stinky smelling stuff she had never tried before but found to be delicious. "Well, we don't have food like this in Indiana! I guess you could say I'm a pretty hardy farm girl" she laughed and dabbed her lips with the napkin.

"As long as you are having fun, then," Zander said as Savannah nodded emphatically. Turning more serious he added: "Sorry I won't be able to see you much in the next few days. It's going to be a big harvest weekend and we've got new equipment arriving tomorrow – it's a destemmer that shouldn't beat up the grapes quite as much as the typical units," Zander explained as his hand traced the contours of her upper thigh, hip, and roved up her rib cage. They had moved to a little lounge area of pillows and a blanket. "But, I'd love for you to come to harvest sometime. Maybe next week when it's little better timing?"

Savannah could feel her desire rising. Zander, despite his slightly funky outfit choices, the odd skull and cross-bones belt buckle and his English over-the-pants riding boots, was still hot. And, it had been a long, *long* time…

"I'd love to."

"Good. Right now I'd love to kiss you," Zander said as he leaned in and gently pushed her to the blanket.

Savannah found herself to be *more than* willing to yield to Zander's advances. He kissed her gently, almost too gently, sending soft, slow waves of desire flowing through her limbs from her shoulders down through her fingertips.

Back at the cottage Zander stood with her at the door. They had walked hand in hand from the stables. Savannah knew Zander and Xave still lived in the main house and that if something more was going to happen, it was obvious he was hoping she would invite him in. He kissed her again, pushing her gently against the doorframe, but Savannah hesitated – and didn't. A look of true disappointment on his face, Zander left. Savannah wished she hadn't felt relief, but she did. The steamy kissing (and more!) up in the vineyard had felt so good that Savannah realized it was good to let her guard down a little and to be swept away again. Just a little swept away though - not Cade Champion-level, out of control, almost terrifyingly swept away. But, she needed to slow Zander down.

As she took off her boots, she noticed her cell phone blinking indicating a voice mail.

"Hey, there beautiful," came the languid, drawling voice of Cade Champion. "Have you decided about coming over to work cows tomorrow yet?"

Savannah found herself smiling out loud, a warm happy feeling spreading along her abdomen.

God, just his voice made her all…

"C-mon, Savannah," Cade continued. "I know you're thinking about it. So, just come out. Let's get to know each other a little more. What harm could come from that?"

That comment made Savannah laugh out loud. Cade was dangerous as a raptor. Maybe she should have asked Zander in so the handsome man on her mind could be him.

Now her nocturnal thoughts went again where they hadn't stopped going since Denver.

Back to kissing Cade Champion.

SEVEN

AN OLD FLAME BURNING

S avannah worked cows every spring and fall through the chutes at home, so giving vaccines, running a headgate, shearing top lines, and pouring on insecticide were nothing new to her in theory, but what she and her dad did was *never* like what she was experiencing in California at the Pedrocelli Ranch! First, there was the sheer volume in number of bovine, yes, but also the noise level! The sound of a hundred pairs all of them bawling for each other and upset at the same time was damn near deafening! She'd never even seen a group of that size all together in one place - probably no one in Indiana had a group of a hundred cow-calf pairs to work one given weekend. Then there was the dust. In California the dryness of the earth was startling, especially compared to the Midwest humidity she to which she was accustomed. By 9:00 am Savannah felt choked with it; in her nostrils, in her eyes, and in her throat was a constant feeling of needing to clear it or get a drink of water. Bits of dust settled everywhere-the crease of her shirtsleeve, across the bridge of her nose as she wiped away a bead of sweat. Cade had given her a bandana to wear around her neck, but even with that, she felt as though she had swallowed half the state by noon.

It was exciting and overwhelming at the same time, being in the Golden state and working, if only for a couple days, on a ranch with Cade.

No, it was surreal, Savannah mused.

As Savannah ran her post at the headgate, she watched Cade moving cows toward the tub and through the corral system. It occurred to her that working cows was the way she had had her very first glimpse of Cade back in January. He was vivid in her mind's eye: tall, capable, a goatee in winter that she realized he didn't wear in the summer, laughing out loud with other guys as he pushed a group of show heifers through the chutes toward their night pens. Cade, then, as he was today, had been so damn good looking, so comfortable in his skin, it made her ache for him. Now, as he feathered back a thatch of his golden brown hair and worked the cows through, he was more serious, his broad brows knitted together in a dark furrow, unlike the way he had been so easy in Denver the winter before. She thought about his hands, the lean, long fingers caressing her hair the night she had cried, the way those hands could be so strong and loving as he pressed her to him…Cade exuded a sex appeal that made Savannah's insides swim.

She wished he didn't.

Suddenly, Cade's eyes met hers. He had caught her watching him and, she might as well admit it, fantasizing about him, too. He smiled broadly and touched two fingers to his forehead in a little salute. Savannah blushed to her collarbones, but she couldn't stop herself from giggling as she averted her eyes.

"Hey! Quit your damn flirtin' if you're gonna be any help!" Hollis yelled. She had almost missed catching the next cow, but saved it at the last minute.

There has to be a way to turn off my mind where he is concerned!

———————— • ◆ • ————————

Selena had packed an absolutely delicious lunch, a feast really, especially for being outside working cows and not at a gourmet Mexican restaurant. While Hollis ate like an ogre, he had either been raised well or had been civilized by Monica (and perhaps Francie) because he broke off early and set up a perfectly proper picnic on the tailgate, complete with a tablecloth. Savannah was impressed. Hollis was already eating his grub while sitting on a wheel hub and it didn't take a genius to notice he didn't require company, not that Cade or Savannah minded.

Before they filled their plates Hollis was already stretching out in the truck bed for a nap.

"Does he get any friendlier?" Savannah asked between bites of the delicious grilled tri-tip. They were taking their lunch at an old picnic table under the shade of a small grove of live oaks.

"Ha! Hollis has a stunning personality, doesn't he?"

"I'll say. I wonder what Monica and he have in common?"

"Convenience, I'd guess, or something like it, from what she's said anyway," Cade began.

Savannah resisted the jealous little snarl that her face wanted to make.

"Hollis worked at the ranch when she and Francie were growing up and I guess they dated some when she was in high school and ended up getting married not real long after that. I figured it occurred around the time that their Dad passed away."

"That makes some sense and I know how she feels, a little, about marrying someone for convenience."

"You ever gonna tell me about it - you being married?"

"Yuck! Don't use that word for the relationship I had with Troy. If that is what marriage is, I'm never doing it again!"

"You are divorced now, right?" Cade asked.

She glared at him and smacked his knee; she knew that he knew she was. "Cade!"

He chuckled. "Fine, so you're not ready to tell me, okay." Cade looked away then, towards the higher smooth hillsides that the cows had come down from. He lightly grabbed her wrist and directed her toward his line of sight. "See that ridge over there, Savannah, the highest one that you can barely see beyond these lower hills?"

She nodded.

"I'm going to take you up there sometime soon. It's beautiful, if we go in the early evening, we'll take a six-pack and on a clear day, we can see the Golden Gate Bridge."

"Really?"

"Yes, really. I go there when I need to be alone, but I'd really rather go there with you," pausing, he added. "Although sometimes it feels like I already have," Cade said softly as he rose, pulling her up with him.

"What's that supposed to mean?"

"It means every time I've been up there, all I can do is look for that bridge and it makes me think about how I'm looking for a way to connect back to you. Now, I think the bridge turned out to be lucky for me."

Cade was standing way too near, he was being way too sincere.

"Hey! Let's get back at it!" Hollis yelled and the spell was broken.

———————•◆•———————

After lunch, they kept up the same roles, Savannah working the head-gate and applying the pour-on, Cade pushing the cows up through the chutes, and Hollis giving shots, ear tagging, and pushing the cows on back toward their calves. Savannah tried to better focus on her work, but her mind wandered some to what Cade had said about her being with him all along, especially when he was alone. It was as if he'd spoken the words she would have said, if she had the courage he did. After a while, Hollis hollered for a short break, giving Savannah a moment to herself, but just as she turned her back, she heard Cade.

"Savannah! Hey! Look alive, that bitch is headed back-"Cade was yelling and running toward her, just was Savannah turned to see a wily black recipient cow barreling down toward her. She'd obviously doubled back to search for her calf – or because she was just plain mean. Savannah tried to scamper away from the 1,300-pound rip, but the cow was in full-on mode and barreled right over her, knocking her off balance and back in the dirt.

"Savannah, can you get up, Babe?" Cade was there, yelling at the old cow to turn back, kicking at her. At first the cow couldn't be dissuaded and Cade flung himself in front of and on top of Savannah. Finally, the sound of the right baby's bawling urged the furious bovine back to her calf, but Cade stayed where he was.

"You okay, anything hurt?" Cade asked, his eyes squinting with concern.

Savannah was out of breath and a little shaken up. She knew that people could get seriously hurt if a cow wanted to keep them down. "I'm, ah, I'm a little scared, but I'm okay."

"Good to hear," Cade whispered with relief and his kissed her forehead. Then, taunting her, he said: "Last time I was laying on top of you we didn't have any clothes on."

Savannah broke off the embrace, rolling out from under Cade, jumping to her feet, and swatting dust away from her backside.

"Thank you for saving me from that cow, Cade." She said sternly as she walked back to her post at the headgate.

Her heart was pounding so hard she was certain she was going to have a heart attack and expire right then and there.

"No more working cows up on the hill today," Cade announced when she returned the following morning and began tying the bandanna around her neck.

"Really? Did I get fired?" Savannah remarked. Admittedly she was a little sore in her left side and shoulder from where the recipient cow had waylaid her. Not working cows was just fine!

"Nope. You're hired and my crappy barn help is being sent on another mission today. Think you can handle working in the showbarn all day with just me?"

Savannah smiled with delight she could barely conceal. "You're on Cade! But, you know I hate the wash rack, so I'm not rinsing a damn thing."

"Good to hear because I'm not blowing out a damn thing, either!"

———————————— • ◆ • ————————————

It had been eights months since she had worked on show cattle with Cade. It was surprising, the easy rhythm they fell into as if they had worked together forever, of course they hadn't since they'd only known each other less than ten days when they first met. Still, at the Denver show before the 'break up', they'd worked together pretty good. Having only been around Eddie since, she was used to accommodating his slow pace, his regular complaints, and his propensity to find regular (very regular) reasons to run to the shop for something. But Cade was efficient and she hoped he could not tell that she was hopping just to keep up.

"Ya doin' good over here?" he asked about 10:45 am. Despite the fans in the showbarn, she had broken a sweat from hustling and running the hot blower over the heifer's hair.

"I'm doing great," she remarked, pausing to brush back a matted piece of hair, most of which she had long since swept into a ponytail.

"Okay, Hottie," Cade said with a wink. "Lunch in an hour or so?"

Savannah turned away with a nod and went right back to brushing and blowing. The calves in California had summer hair, which meant there wasn't that much of it, but some of them were curly and she hated wavy hair on a Hereford. It was just as well Cade had sent his crew off on another project; it was clear they spent little or no time really working hair to improve the look of it. They were probably doing the absolute minimum to get by.

She and Cade made the short walk back to the cottage a little past noon where he proceeded to start up the grill.

"Burger, dog, or both?" he asked as he held open the door for her to head into the kitchen ahead of him. He helped himself to a nice long look at her from behind as she went to the sink and washed her hands.

"Burger, no bun," Savannah said. "Oh, there's my phone-its Eddie, I better chat with him."

"Well, how's your excellent herdsman doing?" Cade asked as he handed her a big glass of iced tea.

Savannah sat down and watched Cade flip the burgers, sipping the tea. "He's Eddie-you met him-but actually, lately he's been in a pretty good mood!" In answer to Cade's raised brows she added, "He's got a woman! Now, he hasn't told me that yet, but I've heard her in the background and I've also never heard him so pleasant," she paused, then grinning she added the rest of the story. "I think she's a stripper. Her name is Crystal."

Cade roared with laughter. "Hey, everybody needs to get laid."

"Oh, Cade, but I mean, I cannot imagine screwing Eddie!"

Cade winced. "And, I refuse to imagine that! But, Eddie would love for that to happen some day."

Cade served her lunch – it was *only* a burger and chips but he was a bachelor after all. She noticed he'd brought out the condiments and the pitcher of tea to the porch.

"Please! We're past that and I've never been interested in that. If there's a girl out there for Eddie then I am more than happy, even if she does show her boobs to everybody as a job!"

"Hey, a girl's gotta make a living!" Cade laughed as Savannah scowled at him. "I'm serious! You know, sometimes, that's how guys like Eddie end up meeting women. How's he doing on taking care of your place?" Cade asked, skeptical. Savannah didn't know it, but Clint had kept him up to date and they'd even talked a couple times since Savannah had arrived in California.

"Not bad - never awesome - but fine. Right now I wish he'd get motivated -yeah I know-the 'm' word isn't really his strong suit-but we need to find some cows to put embryos in. It's an odd time of year, but if we start soon we can be getting August and September calves next year. Problem is, nobody around us seems to have any recipient cows - at least not that Eddie has found."

"You know, I've got a group of cows still down at the Bow String Ranch. They'll be weaned off pretty soon. We could work a deal to send the embryos down and have them put," Cade suggested, a little too casually.

Had he and Clint already been conspiring about it?

Savannah had finished her lunch and stood to lean against the porch railing.

She considered it for a moment but it would mean being tied to Cade and he'd have a measure of control over her and her cowherd, *her* business.

What if he runs off again and I don't know where my cattle are?

"Um, it's nice of you to offer, but I'd have to ask Clint, and you know how Eddie is! He figured that he'd have to drive all the way to Texas and haul them back and he'd just bitch about that, so-"

"I get it. You don't think you can trust me, do you?"

"Cade, it's not that, but-"

"Hey, I have work to do to win you back, I get that," Cade was matter of fact. "But, right now we have other work to do - race me to the show barn!" he added by swatting her firmly on the ass and dashing off the porch.

"Cade! I cannot believe you did that!" Savannah tore after him, catching up quickly.

Cade wasn't much of a runner, but then, he probably wanted to be caught. She took her turn slapping his firm backside a move that he rewarded by grabbing her around the waist and throwing her over his shoulder.

"Cade! Oh my God! Put me down right now!" Savannah shrieked and laughed all at the same time.

"Nope! Can't do it-gotta make sure you work for me this afternoon, so I'm carrying you to the barn!" Cade was laughing, too, and smacking her playfully on the butt, in a patty-cake rhythm.

Spooking the tied group of sale heifers as he whooshed her off of his shoulders, Savannah shook herself out like a cat just sprayed with water.

"Cade! You are nuts! You just carried me 50 yards!" she was trying to act put out. What she was turned on…

God I want him…

"Yeah, I did, and I'm out of breath!" Cade laughed and doubled over a minute, hands on his knees.

"Well! You old man!"

"Ha! I may be old, but Young Lady, for a skinny girl, you really weigh!"

Savannah's eye flew wide open and she lunged at Cade. "I do not!"

Cade shied away from her fists. "Hey, you're spooking the stock!" He headed toward the wash rack. "Be back with one for you to blow out in 10!"

She heard his laughter above the hum of the fans.

"Before you go, want to share a couple beers and go with me to see how my crew made out today?"

It was nearly 4pm and they had been working – and flirting - all afternoon. Around 2pm, Cade had washed them all and started to run the necks and shoulders on a few of the heifers. She was mostly done brushing but instead of leaving to go back to her desk at Monica's house, she kept finding reasons to hang around. But, by the end of the day, Cade could tell he wouldn't be able to keep her around much longer.

"Sure," Savannah remarked. "What have they been doing all day, you never said. Something for the barn project?"

Cade grunted a laugh that indicated 'no way'. "Yeah right! I wouldn't let this group of derelicts touch *any* building I'm planning on ever working out of. I sent them up to the corrals where you and I were yesterday to shear some of the better end cows for the sale."

Cade began wiping his Andis-brand shears, cleaning the blades and picking hair from the metal scotch comb as he surveyed his work.

"But, I thought that was what you were doing at the ranch in Montana - shearing cows for spring sales?" Savannah queried.

Cade nodded. "Yeah, I was, but when you shear cows from Florida to Oklahoma, from Oklahoma to Montana, and you're livin' out a your car, eating, sleeping, drinking with the same guys for a couple months," Cade arched one of his full, dark brows, "Well, a man just gets the F over it."

They drove Cade's pick-up to the corrals where Savannah could see the group of 'employees' hanging around, beer cans scattered everywhere and a couple of them napping on top of the old picnic table where they'd eaten lunch the day before.

"F'n jack asses." Cade grumbled a curse. "Worse than I figured. Stay here."

As soon as the group saw Cade, they started in loudly making a bunch of excuses. He kicked the boots of the guy napping, knocking him clean off onto the ground. Savannah felt a little like a voyeur, but she put the window down to listen.

"You idiots got even less done than I expected!" Cade was yelling. She'd never seen him raise his voice. He looked pretty menacing. "That's it - pack your shit. You're all fired!"

Savannah gasped as a beefy man with a ruddy complexion started to come at Cade, but stumbled as he did it. He was clearly drunk. "Champion! You can't fire me!"

Cade was unphased and didn't even raise his eyes as he started straightening up. "Larry, you're wasted off you ass and I just did."

Cade paused long enough to address a greasy looking younger guy that appeared like a drug addict. "Turbo, make sure Larry gets home. And, none of you pricks show up here, again-you hear me?"

Once they left, Cade signaled to Savannah to come out of the truck. She'd actually found a feed sack in the bed and started to help Cade pick up their beer cans and McDonald's bags. She didn't comment until Cade did.

"Well, it won't be long now," Cade remarked as he popped the top of the Coor's Light Savannah handed him.

"What won't?"

"What's bound to happen next. You'll see."

Cade was right. Not ten minutes later came an F-350 diesel flying up the lane, throwing gravel and rocks everywhere.

"Champion! You just fired all the damn crew?" screamed Hollis, pounding his massive fists on the truck hood. He didn't even bother shutting his door; Savannah's eyes widened; she hoped he'd put it in park.

Cade crossed his legs and leaned against the chute.

"Yep."

"God Damn it! What are ya planning to do now, eh?" Hollis stormed around, kicking up dust in his temper tantrum. "One of them guys is my cousin, Larry!"

"Your cousin Larry was the lead drunk on the crew and you know it. His biggest contribution to this ranch was buying the beer for the couple of under-aged low-lifes you hired," Cade said, stretching to his full height and approaching Hollis. "They required constant supervision to keep them off the bottle. Now, I just spent two days NOT hovering over them like a nursemaid and they accomplished the sum total of jack shit."

Savannah sucked in her breath.

Was Cade going to fight Hollis?

She had never dreamed someone could or would be so direct with an employer - especially not one with a mean attitude and the physique of a Cornhusker lineman.

"I'll call the local FFA tomorrow and get us a couple good kids to fill in for a week and then I'll call around to some free lancing friends and put together decent crew," Cade had started to sound conciliatory but Hollis just turned to him and scowled. Cade puffed out his chest a little and then smirked. He knew what Hollis was thinking.

"Hollis, it had about come down to me or them. I was sick of that half-assed group. You hire them back and I'm gone."

Hollis grunted audibly. Champion was right and he knew it. His local cronies were a bunch of boozers, he'd just never had the guts to send them packing.

Suddenly, Hollis turned to face Savannah, his small icy blue eyes beady slits. "And what about you, Miss Author? You seem to know your way around a showbarn. Except for getting your self run over by that bitch yesterday, you're pretty capable," he remarked callously.

Savannah started to shake her head at what Hollis was implying. Cade's smile widened. "The two of you sure have a good 'working relationship,'" he said, using air quotes around 'relationship'. "Monica didn't mention you two had a 'thing' goin' on."

Savannah glared at Hollis. Scared of him or not, she didn't appreciate his attitude. "We do not have anything going on!"

"Whatever you do on your own time is your business, Young Lady, I don't give a damn-"

Savannah cut him off again. "Cade!"

Cade chucked softly, it amused him that even a meathead like Hollis could see they were in love. The only person choosing to ignore that truth was Savannah. Hollis was going to help him out.

"We don't have anything going on, at least not at the moment. But, yeah, we have a history, don't we Savannah?" he said with a wink.

Savannah bristled. Cade was always so damn smug.

Hollis grunted his approval as he nodded in Savannah's direction. "And why wouldn't 'ya? Listen, we're short of help now since Mr. New Cowboy here fired 'em all. So, ah, why don't you just come over a couple days a week?"

Savannah was mortified. Cade had just informed Hollis they had been lovers and Hollis had just offered her a job. She crossed her arms and tucked her lip, her disapproval evident. She glared at Cade. He shrugged 'innocently'.

"Listen, Hon, I'll pay you-you can't wanna sit at a desk all day, anyway, can ya?"

Savannah's anger rose at Hollis's patronizing use of 'Hon'.

"Hollis, that is a kind offer and I'd love to help out, really, I would, but this was a one time thing. Besides, Francie is already paying me to write the book, so I couldn't possibly double dip."

"Ah-that's bull," Hollis grumbled, dismissing her point. "I'll just call Francie, she ain't gonna care, I'm telling ya. She loves this damn place as much as my wife does."

At the mention of the word 'wife', thoughts of Monica with her seductive glances and low cut tank tops flittered across Savannah's mind. She hated to think about that woman with Cade.

Hated it.

Apparently, there was something about which she and Hollis could agree.

EIGHT
TWO WORLDS COLLIDE

"Y es, Hollis called, which in itself is irregular. We don't have frequent phone conversations," Francie remarked.

Savannah was sitting with Francie and Zander on her Westward facing deck that overlooked the vineyards. The sun was beginning to set creating an extraordinary golden-red scene. It was a Friday night and she and Zander had been leaving when Francie stepped out and asked them to come inside for a glass before they went. Savannah figured it was about her working at the ranch as help.

"Savannah, I think it is great! Of course you love the cattle and want do something more physically stimulating while you visit than just writing. I get that!"

"I'm so glad, I didn't at all mean for Hollis or Cade Champion, for that matter, to invite me to do that on a permanent basis, but-"

"But, with my handsome son so busy on the weekends, you absolutely must want something to do! Promise me you'll take him with you - I always hoped my grandchildren would show cattle!"

"Mother!"

Francie sipped her cabernet and smiled smugly. "What? You two think that I think you're just pals going on and picnics in the vineyard? Xave told me what a romantic set up he created - I'm delighted that you're dating!"

"Well, that's a relief," Zander remarked wryly. "Savannah, let's go-"

"No I mean it, Savannah, make sure Zander goes with you and learns about brushing, blowing, leading, all of that. You know with their father being English, my boys and I spent most summers in Europe - I don't think either of them has ever even been to a county fair!"

———— •◆• ————

Zander drove a Porsche - not just 'the basic black' either, but a cherry red convertible. Once again, Savannah *could not wait* to tell Macy. Savannah had spent extra time getting ready for the evening out. They were going to a party at the home of some of Xave's culinary institute colleagues and Zander said it would be a pretty fun crowd. Savannah decided to go shopping and picked up some cute little dresses and heels. She didn't really know what to wear but pulling things together with her hair and make-up, she knew that she looked good. Zander's eyes said as much, too, as they buzzed down the lane and onto Highway 29.

"You know, it's true. I really don't know jack about cattle, sure as hell not about showing them," Zander mused, his hand placed possessively over her kneecap. "As soon as I'm able, I will be over there to work cows with you and Monica's New Cowboy."

Savannah did not like the reference to Cade as a 'possession' of Monica's but choked down any comments that Zander wouldn't understand. There was no way she was letting him work on show stock with she and Cade. That was just way, too, well, *wrong.*

"Zander, its not like it's a big deal at all, they're just cows, you know. I mean you have horses and it's kinda like that. I'd rather spend my time with you doing something fun." Savannah helped move Zander's mind off the subject by nibbling his earlobe.

———————— • ◆ • ————————

The settings in Napa Valley seemed to endlessly trump themselves. What was gorgeous and gourmet in one place, like Kingsley Estate, was always outdone by something even more gorgeous and gourmet at the very next place. They pulled off Highway 29 and onto a frontage road that led up the hillside.

"I think this is the place, but I'm trying this new Tom-Tom and I dunno if these GPS deals really work," said Zander adjusting the big dash accessory that was supposed to yield them directions from the satellite. Driving a little further, a massive gatehouse emerged from the grove of pines. "This has gotta be it," he said as they requested admittance from the guard.

"Really, Xave's friend has a security guard?"

"Actually, this place belongs to the new guy Xave is dating. Apparently it's a real palatial spread."

Zander's Porsche careened up the driveway as it wound around the sloping highlands north of Calistoga. She could see the brightly tiled roof and the fawn-colored turrets above the tree line. The place looked massive. Zander was driving fast, his left hand on the wheel and his right seductively gripping her left thigh somewhere North of her knee. Savannah was enjoying the feeling of doing something completely new. They wheeled up to the imposing Tuscan villa that seemed to completely block out the view of the surrounding mountain. Zander's Porsche was in good company. There wasn't a Detroit-made vehicle in sight. A valet opened her door.

Savannah realized this was an example of what Francie had been called the 'nouvo rich' people. She wondered what Cade would think of it.

"There's my favorite little Cowww-girl!" exclaimed Xave in delight as he greeted them on the porch. "Ian, Baby Boy, come out here this minute!"

Xave demanded over his shoulder as he kissed Savannah on both cheeks. "If you get *any* damn cuter!" Xave grabbed her around the shoulders as Zander shook his head. "There you are, Babe! Isn't Zander's girlfriend just soo, adorable?"

Girlfriend? Is that what Zander is calling me?

Ian/ Baby Boy was a chubby guy clad in a black hooded sweatshirt and baggy jeans with bare feet. Savannah guessed him to be about 35 but it was hard to tell behind his enormous, black-framed glasses. Patches of sparse, scruffy facial hair pocked his face as if they'd been glued on in a poor attempt to create a beard.

"What can I say? Tech billionaire!" Xave waved his wrists as if in explanation as to why he was dating Ian. "I know, I know he's not the hottest too look at but…I mean, this *place!*"

Savannah just giggled to hide the fact that she was a little appalled.

This is going to be either the most interesting or the strangest night of my life.

The home was utterly stunning. Shades of crimson and ochre combined with the copious use of enormous wrought iron work chandeliers and sconces flooded the chambers with light and warmth. A waiter handed her a glass of champagne. Zander took her arm as Xave introduced her to everyone they encountered as though she was a little pet. Ian had already meandered away, completely disinterested in her. Savannah, shrinking back from her usual confident self, was completely out of place.

At some point she got separated from Zander and wandered out onto the overlook. A beautifully set table of appetizers was spread and a white-coated server silently refilled her enormous Reidel wine glass. Savannah was just thinking about indulging in some snacks when a nasally voice rang out behind her.

"Oh. My. God. Do you really have *cows?*, So are they, like, free range?" asked one of the girls Savannah had yet to be introduced to. Apparently Xave had even prepared his friends with her bio.

Seeing Savannah nod, she powered on. "So, well, free range is okay, I mean, it is like an animal *sanctuary* where you live in like Iowa or whatever, right? I mean, well, like *obviously,* you wouldn't even, like, *dream* of eating them!"

This is going to be fun, Savannah thought as she took a deep breath.

"It's not a sanctuary or a zoo, it's a farm. And, yes, certainly we take very, very good care of our animals and yes, we harvest the beef."

The Girl looked shocked and utterly grossed out. Savannah smiled blandly and reached for an appetizer plate but the conversation had attracted the attention of one of The Girl's friends. "Saaash-shaaa! Oh My God! Can you believe that? She eats her own animals, that's, like, um-" The Girl looked to 'Sasha' and wrinkled her pert nose. "like, disss-gusss-ting!"

Sasha likewise scrunched up her nose. "Oh! I know, that's like, eating your own cat - or a puppy!"

Savannah stared at them as if they had two heads. She couldn't resist poking at the simpletons. "Well, apparently you don't mind eating goat cheese?"

The Girl, in mid stroke of stuffing an entire goat cheese and sun dried tomato bruschetta into her mouth, looked confused. "Well, no, I mean its orrr-gaaaaan-icccc, which makes it okay," she retorted. Then looking at Sasha, she added, "Duh!"

A short balding twenty-something guy entered the group carrying two glasses of wine, one of which he handed to Sasha. "Hey, I'm Gabe," said The Boyfriend of Sasha said as he reached down to fill his plate. "So, yeah, I mean, Xave says you gotta a farm or somethin' back in like, what is it, like Idaho, or whatever?"

Here we go again...

"Hi, Gabe, I'm Savannah Morgan. Yes, my family farms in Indiana, actually," she said, absurdly enunciating the word Indiana, as if she were trying to pronounce it to someone to which English, or at least U.S. geography, was a second language.

Gabe looked genuinely interested. "Dude, that's totally cool," then thinking he was making a 'farm-joke no-one-has-ever-heard-before', he added, "So, you look, I mean, like, pretty normal! Yeah, I like figured you'd be wearing a straw hat and have, a like, pitchfork," Gabe laughed and looked around at Sasha and The Girl for support. Savannah gulped back a huge swig of wine.

I am going to just have to get drunk to tolerate these horrible people.

"Eating meat is sooo outdated, and like, you're kinda skinny, I mean not, like real skinny, but decent," Sasha remarked as she nodded in The Girl's direction. "Its sooo, weird, Brittney! Like, eating meat makes you like, fat," Sasha said without a hint of awareness at her rudeness.

She is literally the most ill-mannered person I have ever met.

The Girl, now named Brittney looked equally surprised. "Sooo, true! She's not really that fat. Weird! Eating meat is soooo bad for the environment. It's not politically socially acceptable," she added as if she'd made a very relevant point.

"Do you mean I'm not politically correct or eating meat is not socially acceptable?" Savannah queried. Brittney was the definition of airhead.

Another large sip of wine.

"Dude, come on! Savannah's gonna think we're like giving her a hard time," Gabe interjected. "I mean, I know I shouldn't, but I eat meat sometimes, too," Gabe smiled at Savannah as if they were co-conspirators. "I mean, hot dogs are pretty f'n good! Right?"

"Whatever, that's all still naaasss-sssstteee!" Brittney implored, her nose scrunched up again.

Apparently her grandmother never told her that if she made the expression all the time her face would get stuck like that, Savannah mused.

Gabe patted Savannah's arm as if they were pals, bonded over a secret lust for animal protein. "Hey, its okay. I mean, eating meat is not as politically incorrect as say being a *Republican!*"

The group all laughed hysterically.

"Well, actually, I am a Republican."

The group all looked at her, noses scrunched up in disdain as if she had just passed gas. Amid the looks of shock, Savannah was spared more interrogation by Zander.

"There you are," said Zander as he placed an arm around her waist, then kissed her check. "I see you're meeting some of my friends."

Savannah smiled wanly at Zander. "Um, excuse me, I need to use the restroom." She pulled away from Zander's embrace and stepped out of the room, pausing long enough to let the server add more wine to her glass. The sound of Zander's friends echoed behind her.

"Zander, Dude, like your girlfriend is kinda, like, not cool. She's not even a real liberal, Man," Gabe was saying.

"Oh. My. God, is she voting for, like, George Bush?" Sasha queried.

"Fill her up," Savannah commanded the server as she overheard Brittney.

"That's totally weird you guys, cause like, wasn't George Bush, like *already* the President? Whatever."

Savannah didn't know where she was going just that she was going away from Zander's ag-bashing, uninformed, and flat-out rude friends.

She wished she was with Cade.

The house's great room was overflowing with guests, but Savannah just breezed through, grabbing a full bottle of Cabernet off the butler's table and stumbling outside, down the portico steps and out onto a large patio, but it was crowded, too. She wandered out anyway, spotting below it a few more steps another little patio complete a stone fire pit. A blue-white propane flame burned neatly and there were a set of unoccupied Adirondack chairs.

Savannah flung herself into the chair wishing she'd brought a jacket. She flipped open her phone and dialed Cade.

He answered on the first ring. "Savannah, hey, what are you doing?"

Savannah. God she loved the way he said her name. She took a long, slow sip of wine before she answered.

"Well, um, I'm drinking some wine-"

"Okay, where are you?" Cade's voice registered alarm. "It's loud there, are you at a bar - do you need help?"

"I'm at a party in Napa-"

"Is everything okay? You sound a little drunk, tell me where you are and I'll be there-"

"Cade, I'm completely fine!"

Savannah hadn't considered that Cade would be worried.

I don't sound drunk, do I?

"I went with the Kingsley's-it's a house party, it's actually at the house of the boyfriend of one of the brothers."

"Boyfriend?"

"Yes, boyfriend. One of the Kingsley brothers is gay. The other is a wine maker, but he's really busy with harvest-" Savannah added quickly realizing she had almost walked right into having to explain Zander to Cade.

Cade chuckled a little. "Well, oh, okay. Still, if you need me I can be there in an hour."

"No, no, Cade, don't do that. I'm completely fine. Really."

"I'm happy you called, but you haven't just called me up before. So, what is it?"

Savannah sighed. If Cade were here right now this spot and this bottle of delicious Cabernet would be just so perfect. But life didn't match up perfectly.

"I'm bored, I guess. This place is amazing - I wish you could see this enormous house and they have a security guard and servers and-"

"That shit doesn't interest me. What's on your mind, really," Cade felt his heart starting to race, Savannah was calling him; she had needed him or better yet –maybe she missed him.

Savannah laughed. "I know Cade, that's not you. It's not me either, I guess. The people here, they're just such snobs!"

Cade laughed. "Yeah, people are different out here. So tell me about it, I have all the time in the world for you."

And so she did. Savannah leaned back, savoring the wine and talking with Cade. She had drunk plenty and let her eyes fall closed, the sound of his voice sexy, but soothing.

"Savannah! Hey! I lost you for about half an hour!" Suddenly, Zander was there and she was startled out of her reverie.

"Who is that, Savannah? Who is that man-" Cade's voice was urgent.

"Sorry, I have to go!" Savannah snapped her phone shut.

"Who have you been out here talking to?" Zander looked insulted, like she had ditched him. Which, of course, she had.

"Um, just my Mom."

"Oh, okay, well, hey, I'm sorry about some of those guys, they're all so, privileged. They can be real assholes."

"You don't say?" Savannah remarked with a yawn. "You ready to go?"

Zander probably thinks I'm a real prude, Savannah mused.

She had closed her eyes and pretended to pass out all the way back and at the door she turned Zander away under the guise of being too drunk. Once she lay down in bed, she was restless. Savannah knew she would have to show Zander a little more encouragement than she had lately. After all - she had been the one that had started their fling by kissing him on her first night in Napa! She just couldn't quite bring herself to let Zander in any closer, even though the idea of breaking the 'dry spell' was something pretty appealing. No, she didn't want to loose the opportunity with Zander because he got bored, she didn't want Francie to be mad at her for hurting Zander and she didn't want Cade to know she was (sort of) dating him. Savannah felt stuck. The highlight of the evening had been talking to Cade.

Cade...

All evening she just kept thinking the same thing:

Tomorrow I get to see Cade.

———————•◆•———————

"Just another perfect fall day working alongside my pretty little Barn Bitch," remarked Cade as he surprised Savannah by swatting her on the rear.

"Cade!" she shrieked. "I do not appreciate that term at all!" she shot back, landing a punch to his bicep. Cade laughed heartily as he bent forward and reached for his shears. He picked up a pair, along with a can of oil and clicked them on, testing the blades. "Do you like Barn Diva better, then?"

"Absolutely! I am completely the Barn Diva. Much better!"

Cade stepped in closer to the heifer she was finishing with the blower, taking the metal scotch comb from her hand as he smoothed the hair on her neck and shoulder. Handing the comb back to Savannah, he leaned in to clip the area. As if on cue, Savannah moved around to the other side and continued blowing the hair.

"I need a couple more minutes on this side before you clip her over here," she warned.

Cade's eyes met hers, they were standing just twelve inches apart, the little calf making the natural barrier. Cade's eyes seemed to sparkle as he met her gaze, never letting it go. She could smell his musky cologne-man scent and count the crinkles around his eyes. "I've got all day to wait on you. Besides, I got bored of rinsing and turned it over to one of the new boys." Smirking, he added, "I thought maybe you were getting lonely down here without me."

Savannah grinned and shook her head, as if to say 'no way'.

I love the way her cheeks dimple when she smiles.

"Nope, actually, I was pretty content down here lost in my own little world. I was just thinking through some things I need to get put in the book this next week."

"How is the book project coming? Monica hasn't said much to me about it."

Savannah bristled at Cade's mention of Monica. She wondered what they did when she wasn't at the ranch in the evenings. She pushed her horrid thoughts away.

"It's going really well, actually. It's been a fun project researching it and organizing so far. I've always thought of myself as a writer and that I'd write a book someday, but this project being my first has been a real surprise, I guess."

Cade looked up from concentrating on the heifer's top line. "There have been a lot of surprises in my life, but none like meeting you, losing you, and getting to be here with you again now."

Savannah blushed and tried to turn away. Whenever Cade turned serious he had the power to melt her insides like warm ice cream. "We have been getting along pretty well around this show barn together, I guess I have to admit that," Savannah said with a nervous laugh, trying to play off whatever she sensed Cade was up to next.

"You know, we have, huh? Just like an old married couple!"

"Ha! Hardly! And call yourself old, but I'll never be!"

"You will always be eleven years younger than me, Young Lady, but even you will someday get into your mid-thirties, believe it or not!"

Savannah just shrugged and went back to vigorously brushing a cow-lick on the heifer's off-show-side rib cage.

Cade watched her for a moment thinking about how he hadn't been this completely happy since the day they had met. "Hey, since we are getting along so well, as *you* pointed out, why don't we just go grab dinner in town after we feed?" Cade asked, attempting nonchalance he didn't feel. He had been thinking about how to get Savannah on a date with him for a couple weeks but he was careful not to spooking her; she was as nervous as a green-broke heifer.

"You mean like you and I go on a date?" Savannah's mind was already saying no, trying to remind her of Zander. "I don't think we need to do that, Cade."

"You don't have to call it 'a date' if you don't want to-"

Savannah cut him off. "Well, I don't have anything to wear and my hair-" Savannah attempted to fluff one side of her barn-fan-blown hair to no avail.

Cade waved his hand in annoyance. "Forget that! Come back to the cottage, wash your face and pull you hair in a ponytail while I take a quick shower and you'll be beautiful. "What's the big deal about a grabbing a burger and a few beers? In fact, let's even cut out a bit early. It actually looks like its raining over toward Napa and that will probably blow through here soon, too."

<hr>

Savannah and Cade barely made it to his cottage before sheets of rain pelted them. They had already driven over to Monica and Hollis' house where Savannah ran to her borrowed car. She kept a small bag of provisions stashed in the trunk since her first days of coming over to research the book. It wasn't much more than powder, a hairbrush, a fresh shirt and cut-offs along with sandals, but she figured Cade would be appreciative.

"Wow! This rain!" Cade yelled above the deluge as he grabbed her around the waist and they ran for the porch.

Cade was already shucking off his boots and unbuckling his belt before Savannah could notice. "Cade! What the hell are you doing?"

"No need to drag this damp stuff into the house," he remarked without a bit of modesty. Cade's jeans were in a heap on the porch floor, leaving him clad only in his whitie-tighties and he was already pulling off his drenched t-shirt.

Savannah blushed to her temples at the sight of Cade nearly naked. "I'll go and change first and don't you even think about following me like, like, uh - like *that*!" she exclaimed pointing at Cade's flagrant nudity.

"I'll mix you a drink for when you're done. Crown alright?"

"Make it a double!" Savannah couldn't help herself from giggling.

———————— • ◆ • ————————

"Damn! Nice legs," Cade remarked as Savannah emerged onto the porch. She had put on a tight t-shirt and the pair of shorts and sandals she'd brought along. Cade was sitting there sipping a whiskey and quite obviously pretending to thumb through a breed association magazine. He was still wearing nothing but underwear.

"And now it's your turn to put on some clothes, Mr. Champion!"

"Oh, come on! You telling me you don't like seeing me almost in my birthday suit?" Cade placed a hand on his hip in a ridiculous faux seductive stance.

Savannah laughed out loud and practically snorted her sip of whiskey. Cade was certainly not shy!

"Go!"

Cade's laughter and then the sounds of him singing to himself in the shower could be heard above the din of the rain. Savannah picked up the cattle magazine and was absently flipping through it when a brand new Porsche careened off the main drive and made the turn toward Cade's cottage.

Dear God, NOOO! Don't let it be…

"Hey, Gorgeous! Monica told me you'd be over here!"

Savannah smiled wanly and absently gulped her last sip of whiskey. She had no idea what to do about what was about to happen next.

Zander dashed out of his car and leapt up onto the porch.

"Zander! Uh, hey - what are you doing here? What about harvest?" Savannah was starting to feel nauseous.

"Freaky fall rain storm!" Zander shrugged. "I sent the field crews home and I got to thinking, rather than call you, I'd just surprise you and you could show me about cows!"

Savannah inadvertently stepped back as she sensed Zander coming in for a hug or kiss.

Suddenly, Zander looked confused. "Monica says this is where the hired guy lives. So, what are you doing here drinking a cocktail?"

"I, uh, actually there is a storage room in here with a lot of ranch history that I've been going through on and off."

Zander seemed convinced enough and stepped closer, pulling her into his arms. Savannah wrestled backwards a bit, just as Zander, oblivious, leaned in and kissed her.

"Savannah," came the sound of Cade's voice. "Which one of these Polo's do you like better-" Cade was holding two starched button-downs and wearing nothing but a towel around his waist. His happy grin morphed into shock at the sight on his porch.

Savannah just froze.

"Who the hell is this?" Cade bellowed as Savannah wrestled back from Zander.

Zander stared in shock at the scantily clad man. "Who the hell are you?"

"I'm Cade Champion - and I live here! Savannah, why are you kissing this dude? What the hell is going on?"

Savannah started to explain, to say anything to the two men now both staring at her, but Zander cut her off.

"Well, I'm her boyfriend and my mother owns this ranch!"

Cade looked like he had been hit by a truck. "*Boyfriend*? You have a boyfriend?"

"Cade, I'm sorry, its not, exactly-"

Zander took in the scene. Jeans and shirts, obviously one pair his, one pair hers, were slung over the porch railing. Savannah sitting there having drink like she was accustomed to doing so, and then, the big cowboy coming out in a towel, obviously *not* expecting company. "What's going on with this guy, Savannah?" Zander growled, then, thinking better of it, he threw up his hands and dashed off the porch into the rain.

"Zander wait!" Savannah cried after him. She stepped off the porch, feeling completely torn in two. Zander was already flying out of the drive. She looked back at Cade, the expression on his face breaking her heart. "I'm sorry, Cade, but I have to go."

———————— •◆• ————————

It was just after dawn on Sunday morning as Savannah sat alone on the little deck, a third cup of coffee in her hand. Zander had just left; they'd finally spent the night together and all that went with it. She certainly hadn't planned on Zander staying, but she did owe him an explanation about Cade and the scene at the cottage. So, when he agreed to come in and talk, the hours passed pretty easily. She admitted everything to Zander; everything from having been married before to an idiot to having met Cade and that they had what she called 'a brief fling'. She didn't bother trying to explain the intensity of it or that she had fallen madly in love or that Cade had crushed her heart or that he tried to win her back and she had rebuffed him for the better part of a year – all that was too personal to share. Instead she told Zander the truth that she and Cade had no idea the other would be in California and that nothing had happened romantically.

Zander did not ask her if she loved Cade. Instead he asked her if they could have a chance. It seemed the natural thing to do was to say yes and so the rest of the evening took its course. Being intimate with Zander was, in a word, pleasant. Certainly no fireworks, but fireworks lead to fire, and Savannah wasn't sure she really wanted more of that.

In the morning, Zander was happy and making plans for them. He told her that he wasn't going to stand in the way of her working at the ranch or writing just because an old acquaintance was there.

Savannah pondered what to do about Cade. The thought of not seeing him or not getting along with him while she was in California was just too crazy. She owed Cade an explanation, too. And, she had told him she'd help on the weekends and knew he was understaffed. So, in the end, she got up and took a shower. She was headed back to the ranch to clear the air.

———— •◆• ————

Savannah rehearsed the speech she would give Cade all the way from Kingsley's to the ranch. She practiced how she would tell him she was sorry for not being forthright about Zander and that she truly was having a good time being around him, but yes, she and Zander had 'kind of' started dating. Nothing serious - she would assure Cade - just some fun. Besides, she would remind him, it wasn't like she came to California expecting to reconnect with him after what happened. She thought through how she would tell him that maybe they could just stay friends and it wouldn't be that long until she left anyway, so they should get along. Yes, Savannah, had prepared a plan to deal with the 'Cade situation'.

At the showbarn, only the two FFA boys were in sight; one rinsing, one blowing out the first calf. Neither one seemed to know where Cade was, just that he'd 'be back later'. Savannah called his cell, but he didn't answer. At first she stood idly trying to figure out what to do. Maybe he'd just run an errand or two and would be back, maybe he thought he was punishing her, she didn't know. Eventually, she set to working on the hair after the young guys rinsed and did the first half of the blowing on the sale heifers. Surely he would be back in time for lunch, she rationalized as she tried his line again. But he didn't show up. By 2 pm Savannah was hot, starving, and pissed off. Cade was deliberately ignoring her. Maybe she did deserve it, but it was no way to act. Finally, she tried his cell one last time and getting voice mail, she slammed the phone shut and stormed off in the direction of his cottage.

Cade was there, seated right next to Monica, proofs of the sale catalog scattered across the tabletop as they poured over them, their heads *way* too close. Cade didn't bother looking up, but Monica smiled smugly, like a queen bee protecting her throne. She wore one of her snug tank tops and cut-off shorts. Her long lean legs were tight and tan. She had slipped a sandal off and had a bare foot tucked up under her knee.

Evidently she's pretty comfortable.

"Monica, I'm sorry to interrupt, but I need to speak with Cade," she began, trying to hide the quaking in her voice. She came to the ranch to reconcile, but now she felt her anger rising.

Cade leaned back and placed his hands behind his head. He looked older than she'd ever seen him. He hadn't shaved. "I didn't figure I'd see you here today."

"Well, I told you I would be here to help and that's what I've been doing all morning down at the barn!" Savannah seethed. "Apparently, you haven't come out of the house yet."

Cade's dark brows widened in surprise at the caustic tone to her voice.

"I worked with your high school crew all day. I'm heading back-"

"Back to the boyfriend you conveniently never mentioned to me?" Cade sneered.

Monica began gathering up the catalog images. "Seems like we should finish reviewing these another time, Cade," she purred. "You two have more to talk about."

Monica took her time as Savannah stood, knees locked in rage. She had planned to run off, but she was just so pissed she felt rooted as a tree. A fight was brewing with Cade and she was going to have it.

As Monica slunk past, Savannah swore she could see her smile in delight.

I am really beginning to despise that woman.

Savannah approached the porch. "Cade, I came here to talk with you-"

"Are you sleeping with him?" Cade asked flat out, catching Savannah off guard with the directness of it.

"That is not your business!'

Cade swore under his breath, throwing the glass of iced tea he'd been drinking across the porch where it shattered, sending amber liquid down the steps. He raised his voice.

"Just answer me, because I've about made myself completely insane last night thinking about that scrawny asshole crawling all over you. Are you having sex with that Kingsley boy, Savannah?"

Savannah demurred. "He's not 'a boy', his name is Zander-"

"I don't give a shit what his name - tell me the truth!"

"Are you screwing around with Monica?" The words fell out of Savannah's mouth before she could think it through.

"What?" Cade actually looked surprised. "Of course not!"

"You too looked awfully close to me!" Savannah spat back.

"You're just trying to change the subject. There is nothing going on with Monica," Cade said firmly, adding for emphasis, "Nothing."

"I don't believe you. I see how she looks at you-"

Cade sighed, he did not expect this to turn into an inquisition of *him*. "Listen, I get it. Monica's a flirt, and she shouldn't act that way, but she does. I just try to avoid it."

"Yeah right!" Savannah scoffed.

"Hey, there are Monica's around every corner. If a guy wants to get a reputation like that, he can, but I don't need that kind of rap following me around even if I didn't want you, which I do. It's not who I am."

"Whatever, Cade. You can do what you want!" Savannah said unkindly, as if to show that she didn't care.

Cade was growing tired of the Monica topic. "Listen, Monica is a shit stirrer and she's jealous of you and I-"

"There is no 'you and I', Cade!" Savannah screamed.

Cade threw his hands up in the air. Savannah would not listen to reason.

"There could be if you weren't so damn stubborn about nothing!"

"Nothing?" Savannah shrieked. She couldn't believe his nerve! As if there had been 'nothing'! "You call ditching me in Denver without a word - just - *nothing*?"

"No, that's not what I mean. What I mean is that we have another chance, Savannah. I want you and I to be together!" Cade started to approach, but she stepped back.

"No! It's too late for that. I'm going to date Zander."

"If you don't care about me, then why didn't you tell me about him? Huh? At least answer me that - I know you must still care because in Denver you didn't mention your ex-husband because you were afraid of what I would think of you. So, Savannah, why does it matter what I think about you and Zander?"

Cade had her cornered. "I don't know, Cade! I don't know!" Savannah's sobs came in heaps now. Cade instantly softened

"Savannah, I'm sorry I yelled. I'm just crazy for you. I can't-"

"Stop it, Cade! It's too late! All we had were a few days together and then you were gone! I have spent most of a year getting – no *trying* -to get over you! I can't just go right back to your bed!"

"Oh! So you just decided to find some other random dude to shack up with?"

Savannah's eyes registered hurt. Cade immediately regretted being coarse with her but his heart was burning a hole in his chest with a flame he couldn't put out.

Savannah left.

NINE
HE KNOWS ME, HE KNOWS ME NOT

Cade's sleepless night yielded him only one answer. He needed to see her. He'd been an asshole, again, and even though he thought his question was fair, he shouldn't have yelled at Savannah to find out what was going on. If he was going to get her back yelling and demanding of her was not the way to do it. Problem was now that she had 'a boyfriend' his mind was eternally in the gutter about what might be happening over in Napa Valley. He needed a different approach, so he decided to be kind and convince her to be at the ranch as much as possible. If he could just keep getting her around him, he'd have time to figure out what to do about Zander.

By chore time, Cade had called Savannah three times and she hadn't answered him; he knew she wouldn't. He headed to the cottage for a shower.

Cade was driving into the Kingsley Estate lane just as Zander was picking up Savannah. He had a special date planned for her at the uber-fancy Meadowood Country Club; he was not at all happy to see a red Ford F-250 with a cowboy in it as he pulled up.

"What the hell is he doing here?" Zander grumbled as Savannah looked up with a gasp. Cade was approaching with his long strides. "I'll get rid of him."

"Zander! Don't!" Savannah clamored to get out of the low-riding sports car in her dress and heels.

"You've got a lot of nerve showing up here since I know Savannah has told you about us!" Zander stood to his full height, his arms crossed as he stayed positioned behind the open door of his Porsche.

"Listen, I didn't come here to piss you off, Kingsley. I just need to talk with Savannah for a minute-"

"Get the hell outta here before I call the cops!" Zander spat.

"Zander! That is not necessary. Give me a few minutes with Cade, okay?"

Savannah went to Cade as Zander slumped back into his driver's seat, pouting.

Cade warmed inside to the though that Savannah *did* want to talk with him. She looked incredible in the short white dress, her long, shapely legs gleaming with some kind of bronzer. Her hair was pulled up on the sides. Cade fought the urge to pull her into the truck and drive off.

"Savannah, I just wanted to say I'm sorry for the other day."

"You didn't need to come all the way over here."

"Yes I did, I had to see you. And, you've gotten out of the habit of answering my phone calls again," Cade said, trying to make her smile.

Savannah looked down, then she gently grabbed Cade's wrists and met his eyes. "Cade, I don't want to fight. I should have told you about Zander, I guess. It just wasn't something I thought would be permanent, so, I-"

"Don't stay then, come back with me right now," he gripped her hands firmer.

"No, Cade, I'm better off staying over here until the book is submitted."

Cade sighed heavily. He wanted to scream at her for resisting him, for resisting *them*, but he promised himself he'd play it cool.

"Okay, I'd like to say I understand but I don't. Just don't avoid me or the ranch. Come back and we'll just take it one day at a time."

Savannah nodded and started to step away, but Cade pulled her close and kissed her forehead, then whispered against her hair.

"He's wrong for you and we both know it."

———— • ◆ • ————

"Zander, come out and sit with me a minute. I'd like to hear about harvest," called Francie from her veranda.

Zander pulled a nice Cabernet from wine fridge in the office and stepped outside. It was only mid-evening and after he and Savannah had gone to dinner in Napa, she didn't invite him in. He'd been wandering around the main house considering some paperwork and a glass of whiskey when his mother heard him.

"So, harvest is about as expected, though we're delayed a couple days due to that rain we just had," Zander began as he eased into the leather chair. It was a beautiful California evening, cool enough for a jacket and a fire, but warm enough to linger. He wished Savannah hadn't been so aloof.

"That's good, Dear, but actually I had another question for you," Francie sipped her wine and adjusted the blanket around her shoulders. "What was the ranch's hired man doing here yesterday?"

"Oh boy, yeah, that's thrown a wrench in my life," Zander quipped dryly.

"What's going on, Son?"

Zander blew out a big puff of air and leaned forward, elbows on his knees.

"In a shitty stroke of complete coincidence, apparently he and Savannah knew each other before, and, well, they have had a relationship in the past."

Francie's brow raised, at least to the extent it could given her recent Botox ™. She hadn't anticipated competition from the help. "Oh my. Well, it's over with them, right?"

"Savannah assures me that it is. I guess he showed up here yesterday looking to apologize. She hadn't mentioned to him that she and I were dating and when I surprised her at the ranch yesterday, he was certainly not expecting to see me kissing her," Zander paused to sip.

"Oh, damn!" Francie gasped.

"Yeah, I guess she wanted to avoid telling him and he was pretty upset. I suppose he thought maybe they could hook up again or something-"

"Zander, don't use such tacky vernacular," Francie snapped.

"Sorry, Mother. Anyway, she talked to him a minute, told him to go home and we went out. I'm not sure what else to do," Zander sighed.

Francie was disgusted at her son's lack of will power. "Alexander Jefferson Kingsley! You are just lazy! I thought you really liked this girl."

"I do, but, I mean, if she wants him-"

"Nonsense! Girls always like cowboys, it's a natural rite of passage, but you offer her so much more. For God's sake, put some serious effort into winning her heart! I suppose this lack of initiative is my fault. You and your brother never having to work for anything-"

"Mother!" Zander stood to leave. She was chastising him about how to be more effective at getting a woman in bed. "This conversation is ridiculous!"

"It is not! Listen here. We both know I'm only ever going to have the chance for one daughter-in-law and I adore Savannah. She's beautiful, talented, hard working, and grounded and with a little more time and polish will also fit in nicely here, too. You have resources at your disposal, your life has provided those. For once, take the initiative!"

Savannah spent the entire week at Kingsley Estate. Her time was enjoyable and she had good, productive days spent doing a lot of writing and editing. Working for hours alone had actually lifted her spirits and she began to envision what it might be like if she were a 'real writer' working on a book project all the time. She and Francie had taken to meeting daily for a long lunch where she shared the results of the draft and Francie reviewed her work from the day before providing comments and filling in factual details. Despite her constant involvement, Francie and Savannah got along well and Savannah truly liked her. She would miss being around Francie when she went home.

Zander was predictably busy with his harvest duties and that actually suited Savannah just fine but he came by the guest cottage every evening regardless of what time he ended the day. They shared dinner if it was early enough, otherwise she dined with Francie. Zander wanted to stay, but after the first night that he did, she resisted his request to spend the night. She just felt weird waking up with him there.

Friday evening, she, Zander, and Francie were at an art gallery opening and fundraiser in Napa. The California sparkling wine flowed freely and the crowd represented all the biggest names in the wine industry. Francie had even introduced Savannah to the editors of *Wine Spectator* magazine and they appeared to be enamored with her book project, or at least they were polite enough to Francie to act like it.

While Savannah had gotten a lot accomplished during the week, she did need to get back to the ranch for more material.

If she let herself admit it, she also needed to see Cade.

She thought about calling him all week on and off, but resisted it. What did she have to say to him? 'I'm sleeping around with Zander and having a lot of fun, but oh yeah, what I'd really like to do is being blowing out cows with you?'

That made a hell of a lot of sense.

Savannah was starting to feel blue and bored with Francie and Zander's crowd, so she slipped out onto the patio for some air just as her cell rang. As if he'd read her mind, it was Cade.

"Hey, there," he said, his voice low and soft.

"Cade, hi, I was just thinking about you-" Savannah could not believe she let that fall out of her mouth.

Cade chuckled. "If I called you every time I thought about you I wouldn't have gotten any work done this week," he paused then added: " Did you get a lot of writing time in since you haven't been back to the ranch?"

"I did actually, but, I am going to need to come back over, so that's why I was thinking about you, it was just that, I, well, I thought I should let you know. In case-"

"In case I try to talk you out of dating Zander again?" Cade drawled. "I'm not going to do that. I don't think you should date him, but I don't want to fight you. I just miss being around you. I'll be honest, I've been lonely all week."

Savannah's insides started to turn to mush.

Cade Champion misses me...

Cade went on. "Besides, Hollis' offer still stands. I sure like it when you hang around the showbarn and give me a hand," he admitted, then hoping to add the carrot, he added, "And, remember when I told you that we would be doing a round up soon? Well, that starts tomorrow. You don't want to miss that do you?"

Cade wants me there. Savannah could feel her resolve waning.

"Well, like I said, I do need to get more material from the storage room, but-"

"Can't you just admit that we have fun together and come back?" Cade's voice actually sounded desperate.

"Savannah! Hey, I wondered where you were!" Cade heard Zander announce. "Oh, I see you're on the phone-who is it?"

Cade bristled. The little jerk was taking her away from him again.

"Cade, I need to get going. I'm at this event with Zander and Francie. But," Savannah lowered her voice, "I'll see you soon."

Cade hung up his cell and let out a whoop.

"She told Zander it was me!"

If Savannah didn't lie to Zander about the fact that they'd been talking, then he must have heard her say that she was coming back to the ranch.

To see *him*.

Not so fast, fancy boy. She's not yours yet…

———————— •◆• ————————

"Why were you talking to the ranch hand?" Zander sneered.

It was the first time Savannah had seen him drunk and she was surprised at how hateful he sounded.

"His name is Cade and he is the show and sale cattle manager, not a 'ranch hand,'" Savannah shot back. "I let him know that I would need access to his cottage storage room again. I've been planning all week to get back over to the ranch anyway."

Zander leaned against the patio railing for support.

He's damn drunk.

"Well, you can't just go over there now unsupervised."

"Excuse me? Unsupervised? *Really,* Zander?" Savannah decided the evening was over. Francie had already left and now she was going to have to drive Zander back.

"Well, yeah, I mean, I get that you gotta do the book project for mother and Monica, but its not like you need to be cattin' around in that dude's cottage again without somebody else there."

How dare Zander think he can tell me what I can and can't do!

He obviously didn't know her very well. "Zander, come on, let's get you home, this conversation is over," Savannah laid her hand lightly on his arm. She was frothing mad on the inside, but frankly, she just wanted away from Zander, so faking nice seemed the quickest route to being alone.

"Sure, I'm ready if you're ready," Zander slurred obliviously. "But, I'll tell mother and she can accompany you tomorrow if that's what you really need to do."

Savannah rolled her eyes, unable to resist upbraiding him. "Besides the book, I like helping out around the barn and I'm a little bored when I don't. I grew up on a cattle farm, Zander and that's who I am. And, tomorrow we're going to round up some cows in the hills. I'm missing the farm and being over there just feels right. But, I wouldn't expect you to understand."

TEN

THE ROUND UP

Z ander apologized for being a drunk jerk by sending up an elaborate breakfast in bed complete with mimosas, balloons, and two dozen roses. How he managed to pull off something like that in about 12 hours, she had no idea, but when Savannah let him in the cottage, it was easy to forgive Zander.

"What are you up to today?" Savannah queried taking note of Zander's equestrian boots, vest, and oddly shaped cowboy hat.

"Well, I'm going with you to the ranch, of course!" Zander announced smugly as he sipped his mimosa.

Savannah was sure she hadn't heard correctly. "What do you mean-"

"I called Aunt Monica and she told me that today is a big round up day where they are bringing cows down from the hills – you didn't tell me that last night, or," Zander looked sheepish, "if you did I was too drunk to catch it. Anyway, I wanted to be a part with you, so I'm loaded and we're both going!"

Oh. No.

"Zander, that's ridiculous!" Savannah shifted uncomfortably. "You're in the middle of Cabernet harvest. You really don't have to do this-"

Zander was already standing. "But I want to! I've even got my saddle and a saddle for you loaded. Come on, we're going,"

Savannah objected once more but followed Zander outside where he opened the back hatch of his Range Rover. Two western-style saddles and gear were loaded.

"Zander, you won't need this. I mean, Cade, he'll want to move cows on 4-wheelers-"

"Monica said the remuda horses could be used if we wanted to and I'd rather ride. I packed Mother's saddle for you!"

Savannah stood in indecision for a moment.

Cade was going to be furious. She considered calling him.

"Let's go!" Zander was already behind the wheel, squirting Visine into his bloodshot eyes.

On the drive over, Savannah tried to rationalize all the ways that Zander crashing the round up could turn out fine. She wasn't able to come up with any. She thought again about just calling Cade and telling him what was about to happen, but couldn't see a way that her doing so while she was with Zander wouldn't lead to a fight. Zander seemed so delighted, maybe he just wanted to make her happy and maybe it wouldn't be a big deal.

Zander really wasn't at fault; he just didn't understand her life. How could he? He had not been raised around cattle showing. Still, while she was in California, he was fun to be around and with last night as the one exception, he had treated her wonderfully. Maybe it would be cool to ride horses while they moved cows-it wasn't like she ever did that in Indiana. She resolved that she wouldn't bother getting upset with Zander about things that just weren't part of the world she and Cade knew.

———————— • ◆ • ————————

"You've got a lot of nerve bringing your fancy-ass boyfriend over here for this," Cade growled at Savannah. Zander was busily unloading his saddles and had followed Monica to where the ranch horses were tied promising to select a gentle one for Savannah.

The summer pasture – if you could call the brown bits of grass pasture - was an hour from the main ranch. Savannah and Zander had met the rest there. She hated that Cade was angry, but her ire was up, too. He just *assumed* it was her fault.

"Hey! I had no idea this was happening. It's not like I invited him!"

"Really? Well, this is just great, then, Savannah. Just great. I get here this morning and Monica and Hollis have got these damn nags all wrangled around and I'm like 'what's all this about' and she says 'your girl is bringing Zander and he wants to ride, so I told him he could'. So, then, because you decided to make this into to party, my day has just turned into a goat-roping!"

Savannah was furious at his attitude. "Cade, I tried to talk him out of it, but he's so jealous about you and I working together that we had a fight last night and this is what it resulted in!" She paused then, not sure where she was going with it next. "We'll leave if you don't want me here-"

Cade grabbed her arm a little too roughly. "You know I want *you* here. But, I don't want that damn baggage you're hanging onto here!"

"Champion!" Zander yelled out as he galloped over. "Take your rough hands off my girlfriend!" Zander was leading an old-looking mare for Savannah.

Cade rolled his eyes and swore as he started to stalk off toward his 4-wheeler.

"What's the matter? Not cowboy enough to ride a horse?" Zander sneered at him as he attempted to help Savannah with her new mount.

"Zander! That's enough!"

Cade turned on his heel and gave Zander a look that could cut glass. "If you f-up one thing on this round up, I'm coming for you, Kingsley. Keep out of the way. You're here on a leisure tour, but this is work for me." Cade turned away and instead of getting on the 4-wheeler, he walked to the remuda.

"Cade, you don't have to do that!" Savannah called after him but Cade ignored her.

———————— ◆ ————————

Though it was fall, with the brilliant sun on the open ridges the morning soon turned hot. Savannah had long since pulled her hair into a ponytail and put on a ball cap to shield her face, but with the wind whipping her hair, she couldn't keep the long tresses out of her face. Riding wasn't her strong suit and she needed her wits about her, so finally she made a bun out of her hair at the back of the cap.

The air was dry and scented with a dusty floral foliage Savannah couldn't name and the occasional hint of sea air with a blast of coolness would waif past as they rode. The terrain was more rugged and not as beautiful as the lower, rounder hills by the ranch. While there had been a few small live oak groves when they first set out, now the area was dotted with rock outcroppings and the occasional small, scrubby trees that seemed nearly devoid of leaves.

They didn't see a single cow for the first hour but Hollis had told them they probably wouldn't because the herd would be farther afield and actually closer to the end point, still they covered the ground looking for strays.

The land was so rocky and windswept that Savannah wondered what there had really been up there to eat all summer anyway. The plan was to round up the group and push them to the holding corrals where the pairs would be loaded onto trailers. Back at the ranch, Cade would sort out the best cows and calves to include in the sale and the rest would be culled.

The ride hadn't been going well, but it hadn't been going terrible, exactly, though tension between she and Cade and between Cade and Zander was evident. Cade had come by and asked her if she was riding okay, (she was, albeit a little nervous) but then, he just scowled at her and took off when Zander approached. It completely annoyed Savannah that Cade was being so bullheaded. She didn't invite Zander and hadn't wanted him to come, but apparently Cade decided to believe otherwise.

Savannah watched Cade on horseback with interest. He looked incredible, his long limbs taught along the flanks of the big roan, his back straight and broad, but she could tell that he wasn't particularly confident. Savannah realized some of his frustration was that riding was slowing him down since he didn't commonly work cows from a horse. Still, that was his fault; there were two other hands that had come along on 4-wheelers. Zander on the other hand acted glib and showed off his riding skills. At first Savannah *was* impressed and having fun with him, but Cade was so pissed about it that and so obvious about the fact that he was mad, that Savannah grew tired of the men's preening like a couple of dumb peacocks.

Most of the cows had been gathered by the time Hollis ordered a short pause for sandwiches and cool drinks. Monica made a show of attempting to lift one of the heavy coolers off a 4-wheeler and when Cade stepped over to help her, she was all too happy to bend forward so deeply that everyone could see down her tank top all the way to the waist of her jeans.

Savannah rolled her eyes and scrunched up her nose at Monica's absurd ploy for male attention.

"Champion kinda likes Monica, huh?" Zander jabbed at Savannah.

She turned and walked away from his remark, hoping he was wrong.

Hollis called for the group to come together. "For those who ain't done this trip before, we're gonna drive these rips a couple more miles, collect the rest of them, and keep 'em together. We're not real far from the chutes. But," he paused for emphasis and looked at everyone more intently. "we'll come to a final hill and as we head down, there's a road we gotta cross. It ain't usually that busy, but semis like to use it to cut across the county. So, you gotta be careful of spookin', alright?"

Everyone remounted and began to scatter out, taking the places that Hollis and Cade assigned them to keep with the herd. Savannah rode alone for a few minutes, Zander had spread out and was picking along a trail, not paying particular attention to his flank of the herd, but Cade had assigned him an area where he could keep watch, too.

"Hey," Cade said as he rode up. "You're not doing too bad out here."

"Hey, yourself," Savannah said with a sniff.

Cade shook his head. "I'm sorry, I've been acting like-"

"A horse's ass, perhaps?"

Cade grimaced. "Appropriate word. Hey, I'm not trying to be a jerk-"

"But, still, you have been," Savannah quipped, not ready to forgive him.

"Yes, I have. I get it. I just hated having him along."

"I know, I really do. I didn't want Zander's lack of cow-sense to spoil the day. But he'll of had his fill of this so tomorrow I'll come work in the barn with you a while and we'll catch up and hang out, okay?"

Cade smiled wanly, feeling like a second fiddle, as if waiting his turn. The sale was now only weeks away. Cade wondered what he was going to do to turn things around with Savannah before she finished the book and tried to leave his life again.

"Yeah, that's great, but in the mean time, tonight you'll go home with him and I won't be able to sleep thinking about it."

Savannah sighed. She didn't want Cade *not* to want her, she just didn't want to give up Zander when she was over in Napa. She had just lamented to Macy earlier in the week that it would be great if they could just stay neatly in their respective parts of her life! Macy laughed and then reminded her that she really was asking *just a bit* much.

Savannah decided a little flirting would cheer Cade, so she gave him one of her melt-your-heart-in-my-hands smiles. "I have been having fun riding a horse like a real cowgirl, though!"

Cade could see she was enjoying the day despite his – and Zander's - actions. Sometimes Savannah was just so cute and childlike that it delighted Cade in a way he never thought he could feel about someone.

He rode closer and grabbed the saddle horn of her mount. "Yeah, and you're looking mighty sexy, too!"

"Hey, Champion! You too busy flirting with Savannah to keep track of these cows, huh?" Zander called out as Cade was looked up to see a pair doubling back about thirty yards away. "Don't worry, unlike you, I know how to ride!" Zander cackled. He was closer to the pair and Cade could see he'd taken the notion that he could spin them back. He'd spent most of the day ambling along, thankfully not helping. He'd picked a bad time to decide he knew range cows.

"Damn him!" Code swore. "Hey, Zander! Let me do that!" Cade hollered as he took off. Zander had already spooked the cow by running right at her head. The move resulted in the pair scattering farther away and then the calf went running in the direction of the hill's edge and the road. Then, Zander found himself surprised as the cow put her head down and charged the horse. For a moment Cade waivered, but as the calf ran toward the hill's edge, Cade loped after it trying to reunite the pair before the bawling cow upset the rest of the herd.

Savannah would later recall how fast everything happened next. She sped up, thinking she should somehow help Cade, but he was already over the hill in pursuit of the calf. On the road, a couple of semis approached attempting to pass each other just as the calf headed into their path.

Savannah's heart quickened as she reached the edge and watched Cade trying to then get the startled calf out of harm's way. The semis blared their horns with nowhere to go. The calf skittered out of the way just as Cade's mount reared up and threw him. As the trucks thundered past, Savannah screamed as she watched Cade roll into the ditch.

Savannah literally dropped the reins and flung herself from the horse and raced, stumbling and falling, down the hill to Cade's side. Somehow Hollis and his mount had reached him quicker. Cade was face down. Hollis was gingerly asking him if he was awake or could move.

"Cade, oh my God! Are you okay?" Savannah flung herself to the ground beside him. She was sobbing as her hands touched his back; he was covered in gravel, dirt, and clumps of grass and weeds.

"I hurt too bad to be dead, so I guess I'm not," Cade managed.

Hollis snickered. "Ah, good, we don't want ya dead, Champion," he said, then added. "Savannah, just relax and sit back. I'm gonna turn your lover boy over real easy like."

More gently than Savannah imagined he could ever be, Hollis laid his hands on Cade and began to roll him onto his back. "I'm just gonna turn you over and get your face outta this pile of cow shit you're laying in," Hollis said, making light. "Don't you move a muscle, man, let me do the moving."

"Aahhh!" Cade groaned and tried a scream of pain but didn't have the lungs to get it out.

Savannah was frantic. "What hurts Cade? Oh, Hollis! How bad is he?"

"Easy, there. I said DON'T move!" he reprimanded as Cade squirmed a bit. "I'm gonna poke a round a little bit here," he said as he lightly touched Cade's ribs, a move that incited more painful cries from Cade. "You've broke some ribs, for sure. Lay still and let's see that arm.

Just then did Savannah notice Cade's wrist was covered in blood mixed with gravel and dirt.

"Savannah, here, take what's left of his shirt," Hollis instructed as he ripped a big piece of the tail of Cade's untucked shirt and handed it to her. "Nice and gentle wrap this on that wrist and hold it to compress that bleeding, but don't rub and don't pick that gravel." He spoke to Cade. "We'll get you to a doc that can see to that. Savannah, you just stop it so he don't bleed some damn much."

Savannah sniffled and did as she was told.

"So, it takes me falling off a damn horse for you to try and get me naked, huh?" Cade joked, then grimaced at the effort of speaking.

"Sshhh, just be quiet if it hurts," she said, then without thinking she started plopping soft kisses on Cade's brow, forehead, and cheeks. "You'll be okay, you'll be okay," she was saying just as Zander and Monica reached them.

"I've already called the EMT's on my cell. It's gonna be 15-20 minutes at least from where we are, but they're on the way," Monica said. "Cade, how are you?"

Cade grunted, "I'll be fine."

"He's beat up, but he can move his fingers and toes, so he'll make it," Hollis got to his feet. "Aw-right, then, good," he dusted his knees and pant legs. "Well, let's the rest of us help them two other wranglers and get these cows in the chutes. No sense letting 'em wander back."

Hollis gave Savannah a hard look. "Do not let him move. If something's sticking out in there, we don't want it poking somethin' important in his guts!"

Monica and Hollis started to their mounts, but Zander attempted to stay. Savannah hadn't noticed him. She was fixated on Cade, her hands were smoothing his hair.

"Come on, Alexander," Monica called. "Believe me, they're not looking for any help from you."

Zander knew she was right. The look of love and concern in Savannah's eyes was not something he had expected to see.

———— • ◆ • ————

Savannah had guzzled three cups of hospital vending machine coffee and was as wired electric line. She completed all his forms and when the nurses assumed they were married, she started to object, but didn't; she wasn't leaving Cade's side and she knew he wanted her there. They'd done x-rays and taken all his vitals and started picking out the gravel and dirt. They sewed up his wrist and forearm-no broken bones - but he got twenty stitches. On his ribs and back he had a few more stitches and his flesh was torn up like a hunk of meat. Worst of all he'd broken three ribs and he was already swelling.

By the time Zander, Hollis, and Monica arrived she was absently thumbing through a trashy magazine while the pain meds had kicked in enough for Cade that he'd finally fallen asleep. Her chair was close to his bed, her right hand draped lightly on his left. Shadows of concern hung grey bags under her eyes and Cade's nurse had even insisted that she take her blood pressure, too. When she got the reading, the nurse demanded that Savannah take some deep breaths, relax, and have no more coffee.

"Savannah, looks like he'll make it, eh?" Hollis joked, not callously.

"The doctor said he will be fine, but that he's really going to have some pain and be laid up with these ribs."

"Yeah, hell of a time for this. Damn it!"

"I know! Cade will be so frustrated-"

"Okay, looks like things are under control here. Savannah, you ready to go?" Zander cut in. They had loaded the stock, driven back to the ranch and Zander had come separately so he could drive back to Napa with Savannah.

Savannah looked up at Zander with a glare. She hadn't yet started to get mad at Zander about spooking the cow that led to Cade nearly being killed. She was afraid of what she might say.

"I need to stay here with Cade."

Zander couldn't hide his frustration. "Savannah, there's nothing more to do here-"

"He's right," Hollis began and surprised her by patting her arm. "You go on back and get some rest. I'll be honest. I'm gonna ask for more of your help with him being laid up!"

"But, I could stay here, tonight-"

"Nah, they'll release him and we'll get him settled in," Monica added.

"Yeah, that's right. Go on home, but be back with your things tomorra. I'd like you to move into that cottage 'cause this man here, he's gonna take some nursing for more than a few days and we don't have time to do it!"

Savannah was stunned.

Move in with Cade?

"I couldn't do that, Hollis!"

Hollis just shrugged. Something told him Savannah would change her mind.

———————— • ◆ • ————————

The night was simply black; shapeless and formless it was so dark. Clouds hung loose and low obstructing any stars that might have been there to light the verdant Napa hills. Savannah sat on the guest cottage deck, chilly despite the coverlet, but unwilling to go back and sleep. Somewhere around 2 am, she realized that the anniversary of her Dad's death was just days away. So much can happen in a year; a year ago her Dad was to be swept from her life and she hadn't known it, a year ago she was still unhappily 'married' to Troy, a year ago she was still working at a soul-killing job and all she had wanted was to quit and raise cows.

A year ago she didn't even know Cade Champion existed.

The day before, on a dusty gravel road somewhere between Sonoma and Marin counties she had almost lost him. The thought chilled her more than the drafty October air.

Savannah had no idea what she wanted. Her life for the last year had been one of confusion and upheaval. Cade and entered her life, exited it, and entered it again. And, in one stupid set of moves by Zander's carelessness, he'd been seriously hurt. She didn't know what she wanted with Cade or if she could trust him or if she was just stupid and should forget all of her fears and go for it with him again. She did know that her own heart nearly stopped beating in the moments she had feared the worst. She had no plan, but by dawn she knew that she wanted only one thing - to see Cade.

———————— • ◆ • ————————

Savannah had dressed and driven out the drive before Zander could come by and see her off. She just wasn't ready to talk with him. She stopped by a diner in Sonoma on the way to the ranch and bought coffees and hungry man breakfasts in carryout containers and drove to Cade's cottage. Ordinarily, at 7 am he'd be at the showbarn feeding, but she figured with his injuries even he would be taking it slow. The front door was open with just the screen was pulled.

"Cade? How you doing?" she called, stepping in.

"Yeah, come on in," Cade called weakly from his first floor bedroom.

Savannah wasn't entirely sure what state of dress he'd be in, but she carried on cheerfully. "I know I'm not real domestic, so I stopped by and got you some breakfast!"

She entered Cade's bedroom and nearly dropped her flapjacks. Cade was sitting on the bed, shirtless, with Monica seated behind him. She was tucked up way too close for Savannah's comfort. One long lean leg hung over the mattress the other was tucked behind his back. She was picking at his bandages where one had seeped in the night.

"What the hell is this!" Savannah exclaimed in spite of herself. She'd spent half the night fretting over him and here he was cuddling up to Monica!

What an ass!

Monica actually looked startled. "He called me and said he needed help because one of these bandages had leaked all over," she said with a sneer. "Is that a problem for you, Hon?"

"Well! I brought breakfast!" Savannah sputtered as she saw that Cade, his ribs and torso swollen out of proportion, couldn't zip his jeans and they lay open, exposing more flesh of his backside than she thought Monica needed to see.

Cade cautiously turned to her in obvious pain and chuckled. "Well, I can still eat, can't I?"

"I didn't bring it for three!" Savannah was still acting like a bitchy woman and she knew it, but the sight of Monica's hands on Cade's naked back made her want to strangle the older woman.

Monica plopped her hands against her legs and stood. She wasn't going to fight the girl over the New Cowboy today. "These are going to need changed twice a day for a while and he's he gonna be coked-out on pain meds for a few days. You gonna be his sweet little nurse day and night now?" Monica slipped out of the cottage with a sniff.

With Monica gone, Cade visibly relaxed. "I'm starving, you gonna let me eat that or have it out with her?" Cade remarked, the teasing, mocking tone of his voice muted, but back.

Savannah wanted to be annoyed at him, but he looked so pathetic and in pain she just couldn't. "Yes, let's eat. Let me help you lean back on some pillows," she said arranging a propped position for Cade and helping him settle back.

"You gonna eat with me?" he inquired. "Sorry, you'll have to join me here-" he patted bed, "I don't have any chairs in here."

Savannah brought the food and coffees and took a seat cross-legged on the opposite corner of his bed.

Cade wolfed down his breakfast with zeal. He'd never been so appreciative of Monica's unwanted advances or a few broken ribs.

—————————— • ◆ • ——————————

Later, she went to check in on the FFA kids leaving Cade to nap telling him that she'd make sure all the sale calves got rinsed and that she would be back with a golf cart in the afternoon so they could go look things over. She spent most of the morning supervising and then went to Hollis and Monica's house for lunch. She probably needed to say something conciliatory to Monica, but she dreaded it. Serena said Monica had gone, leaving Savannah and Hollis lunching together, awkwardly at first, but then they fell into discussing how she could help out given Cade's ribs and wrist.

As Hollis rose to leave, she stopped him. "Well, I, uh, I decided I'll take you up on that offer to stay in Cade's cottage," she spit out, embarrassed. "Is there a bed you can move upstairs to that storage room?"

"Huh," Hollis snorted as a broad smile opened his face. "I already had a couple guys do it when you went to the barn. I figured you'd be wanting to keep an eye on your loving man."

"Hollis-"

"And, I took some towels from the house and put them out there – you know there is only one bathroom in that little cottage. You're gonna have to share it with Cade, but I bet ya don't mind so much."

Savannah blushed to her roots. "Hollis, I'm-" she stammered, but no suitable statement came to mind.

"Savannah," Hollis paused and surprised her by smiling kindly. "I may seem like just a sucker to you, that with the way my Monica acts, but that don't make me blind. Cade Champion is one lucky son of a bitch to have a woman like you love him."

ELEVEN

NEW LIVING (AND DATING) ARRANGEMENTS

The air around them and the space between them had changed.

The first day working with together at the ranch again was a little rough. Savannah and Cade navigated each other cautiously, overly polite and stiff. They had been getting along so well and having a lot of fun - until he found out about Zander. Then, with him getting hurt, his mood had turned bitter; Savannah knew he felt encumbered by his torn up ribs and the pain he had to be feeling, despite the fact that he didn't complain. Cade was undoubtedly beginning to feel pressure since the sale was only a few weeks away. While the doctor had told him nothing would cure his ribs but time, he cautioned Cade not to strain himself and to take rest if he needed it. Of course, that was like telling a bull to ignore a group of cows in heat - Cade wanted to do what Cade wanted to do. The first several days he hurt enough that standing and even breathing were wearing him out but he absolutely would not go back to the cottage and nap and he'd been trying to reduce his pain meds because he said the drugs made him want to barf. The solution came in the form of a golf cart outfitted with several big pillows.

Cade said he felt like an imbecile, but at least when he started to hurt he could sit down while still spouting directions from the seat. The FFA boys had started to avoid Cade since he was 'grouchy' and look to Savannah for directions. She suddenly found herself the intermediary. She truly felt bad for him, so she overlooked his bossiness and the way he was treating her like she was one of 'the help'.

Well, she mostly did...

By the fourth day, she had developed a workable routine of writing after helping with morning chores and then working with Cade after lunch until evening. They were slipping back into the easy banter of being together, but it was different, changing, as they learned little things about each other - like small habits or phrases they used.

All was going fairly well except that Savannah had to stop herself from stealing glances at Cade; she was still so attracted to him that she ought to be embarrassed. At the very least she was annoyed at herself.

Earlier that day over coffee - yes they were sharing coffee together in the morning - he announced that he could feel gravel in the cuts on his back. Before she could object, he doffed his T-shirt and presented his naked back to her insisting she hunt for the offending particles and pick them out. In their brief time together the January before, Savannah never really had occasion to study the components of Cade; the way his shoulders were lightly freckled and that he had a scar from a childhood immunization on his left bicep. While Cade didn't like being held up in the barn, she knew that he didn't mind these moments where they were alone - so very, very alone - and close. Cade didn't press her but he told her just about every morning that she was beautiful and every evening that she looked sexy with a feed bucket.

Savannah pretended that she minded; she didn't.

These moments didn't do much to keep Savannah's resolve that they were not going to get together. More than once she caught herself fantasizing about maybe just sleeping with him one more time before she returned to Indiana…

Irony is an amazing thing. Its said the truth is stranger than fiction, Savannah mused one afternoon.

One of these days I am going to write a novel about this situation….

She was effectively living with one man and dating another.

When Savannah shared that analogy with Macy one evening, Macy absolutely roared with laughter – and then admitted to being rather jealous - she was under strict orders not to tell anyone in the show cattle business although juicy tidbits like this had a way of getting out and *everywhere.*

Savannah knew she was in a 'unique' spot, but even though there was some humor to be had, it felt awkward - no, devious - to be near Cade - they shared a bathroom for Heaven's sakes - and then for him to know that Zander was going to call. So far, she had put him off but he'd been pressing to take her out and so the inevitable 'rematch' between the two completely different men was bound to happen sooner rather than later. Surely Zander wouldn't act like an ass, Savannah hoped, but what Cade would do when Zander arrived to take her on a date, she hated to guess.

One benefit to the situation was that Monica had avoided them and the barn. Savannah had also stopped using the desk in Monica and Hollis' house instead she wrote in the cottage or on the porch with her laptop. Yes, all the cats were out of the bag and everyone sort of knew everyone else's dirty laundry. She hadn't really spoken to Monica since the morning she'd flipped out about her changing Cade's bandages and it was a little strained with Francie, too, for that matter, but since she was at the ranch, she didn't have to own up to seeing her for the time being.

My life is one small serious of disasters, Savannah thought. *And Cade Champion is always at the center of it!*

"Well, it's time to pull my stitches," Cade remarked. The sun had started its descent noticeably earlier than when Savannah had arrived in California almost two months before. She had taken to bringing a light jacket for morning and putting it back on about the time they turned out.

The group of calves Cade had selected for the sale were finally shaping up, putting on weight and hair, their coats gaining a shine from regular brushing and the sweet additives in the feed. As was their evening custom, they evaluated the calves over a beer.

"Cade, they haven't been in there a week!" Savannah was taken aback.

"Whatever. They're heeled enough not to bleed. Plus, they itch. Help me get these out," he said has he opened his clipper box and pulled out a pair of scissors.

"You can't be serious! I haven't ever removed stitches - you need to go to the doc for that!"

Cade gave her one of his looks that could kill, or at least melt, as he arched one big brown brow high and leaned in closer. "Either you help me or I do it myself."

Savannah sighed. "Give me those," she said taking the scissors.

"Where you going?"

"To wash them with hot water and soap. At least I would like to try and not smear dirt and crap into your wounds," she turned toward the showbarn kitchen.

Cade laughed aloud and pulled off his shirt. "That is sweet! Must mean you care about me!"

Savannah shook her head and turned away so she could smile.

"Whew!" Cade jumped as Savannah tugged on a stitch that wasn't ready to be removed. "Ya took a little meat there!"

She instinctively placed her hand on the tender spot and rubbed it. "Sorry! Did it hurt?"

"Well, yeah."

"Well, it's your fault anyway since you are the dummy that wanted these out early. Let's leave this one another few days. You have any alcohol in that box to clean these with?"

"Nah, I'll wash them later when I take a shower, but you could kiss them and I bet they would heal faster," Cade quipped, his voice smooth, low, and sexy.

They were standing as close as two people about to kiss. Savannah's hand hadn't left his back, his hand was laid across her wrist. She looked up at him, meeting his eyes. She felt her insides turn all gooey as her heart palpations started. Apparently Cade gave her a cardiac condition of some kind because it always happened when he was near.

Cade gazed back, taking his time perusing her face, his eyes smiling and warm with little crinkles from facial lines around the corners. She noticed a few grays at the corner of his sideburns that she hadn't seen before. She fought down the urge to touch his face.

"Have I told you how happy I am that you are here with me?" he said, but he made no move to kiss her. "I like working with you all day. You like it?"

Savannah stepped back, breaking off the intensity. "Yes, I admit. It's really been a good week. Mostly, though,"

"Mostly? What do you mean?"

"Well, you are more than a little bossy too me, Mr. Champion."

"Really?" It was clear Cade, typical man, hadn't considered it. "Well, I don't mean to be. How about I take you out for dinner to apologize then?"

Savannah had been dreading this all day...

"I can't tonight-"

Cade drew back, a dark glare clouding his face. "Zander coming over to take ya out, huh?"

"No, actually, I told him I'd meet him in Napa for dinner."

Well isn't that just great."

———— ◆ ————

Despite the fact that Cade sulked the better part of the morning, once he decided to get over it, they'd had a really good day. The showbarn was nearly done but needed some finishing touches to make it workable; brackets to hang fans here and extra hooks for tie-up bars there. Cade came and got her at the cottage about 11 am and asked with her to ride with him to get supplies.

"I'll even change clothes and take you out for a nice lunch as long as you promise not to mention the word 'Zander' the rest of the day," he said. Savannah nodded. Apparently this was Cade's attempt at apologizing.

They rode in his F-250 rather than the ranch truck, spending the hour-long drive talking about what needed to be done in the last few weeks before the sale. He started talking about how to group the calves together in display pens and wanted her opinion on it. When they got back, he planned to enlist her help mounting the new brackets and hanging fans. Not exactly Savannah's idea of fun, but at least the fans were brand new and clean. She hated hanging fans at shows and getting telltale black lines of grim all over her shirt and jeans from hoisting them up. On the way home, Savannah even read Cade a few chapters from her book which he pronounced to be the best book ever.

"You mean you'll actually read it?" she queried.

"Nope. I mean I'd love it if you'd keep reading it to me," he said, then added with one of his heart-stopping grins: "I'm up for a bedtime story any night you want."

"That's why I sleep with the door locked."

"You do? Really?"

<hr />

"Well, look at us, just like an old married couple," Cade remarked smugly. They were eating grilled steaks and salad on the cottage's porch. At some point during the week, Cade had found an old table and two mismatched chairs and placed them out there, moving the grill off to the grass to make room. Savannah had found placemats and colorful paper napkins at the grocery store and put them out while Cade was grilling. The evening air was scented with the comforting smell of cows and the ripe square-bale hay that had been trucked in and stacked for hand feeding the sale stock. Savannah knew she was letting herself play house - a dangerous game.

"Yeah, since I'm older than you, when we get married, you'll be playing nursemaid to me like this the rest of your life."

"Cade," Savannah feigned an eye roll. The porch light was dim. Cade was wearing a freshly laundered long sleeve shirt that was only partially buttoned, it hung untucked over his jeans. His feet were bare and he had showered.

I really, really wish he wasn't so hot...

"You know, you're really a lot better already. You're not going to need me here much longer."

Cade frowned. He leaned back and made a show of rubbing his ribs in pain. "Oh yes I do, these really hurt! I don't think I can even work!"

"Yeah, right."

"Well, you can't leave now, the sale is coming up and besides, you've decided you like me."

Savannah was still thinking of a retort when headlights pierced the purple dusk light and turned toward the cabin. It was Zander's Porsche.

"You invited him here?" Cade growled.

"No, I actually told Zander I'd be working late tonight and that I wouldn't see him until tomorrow or Thursday," she was equally surprised.

"I feel like your Dad. Maybe I should get a shotgun and put it across my lap," Cade grumbled, not at all sounding as if he were kidding. He leaned back in his chair. Cade wasn't going anywhere.

"Hey, Babe," Zander strode onto the porch and lightly kissed Savannah's lips.

"Savannah and I weren't expecting guests for dinner," Cade said blandly.

Savannah shot him a look. "Zander, hey, I didn't know you were coming by-I left my phone in my room-did you leave me a message?"

Zander was annoyed that neither Cade nor Savannah had made a move to get up. "Savannah, I didn't think stopping in to see you was an imposition."

Savannah recovered herself. "It's not!" she exclaimed a little too cheerily. "Um, take my seat. I'll go grab you a whiskey," she grabbed up Cade's glass, but paused. "Well, I guess, I don't know how you take it."

Zander sat peevishly. "I'd rather have scotch."

Cade laughed aloud and leaned forward abruptly startling Zander when he clapped him on the back, a little too hard. Cade winced inwardly when he did it.

Damn ribs!

"Zander, most cowboys I know drink whiskey, so that's what *Savannah and I* have," he began with a fake smile emphasizing 'Savannah and I'. "But, then, you, obviously not being a cowboy, can be excused for not knowing that," he paused and added without a smile: "You're already on my porch, you want a damn whiskey or not?"

"Cade!"

I knew this was going to be rough…

"With ginger ale and plenty of ice, then," Zander said with resignation.

"Sorry, we've got Coke or maybe some flat Seven-Up," Savannah explained.

"Whatever works. Coke, I guess."

"Coke, *please*," Cade said grinding his teeth. "I'd like Coke *please*, Savannah, and thank you."

Zander did not at all like being upbraided about manners by Cade Champion, a man he didn't consider to have any culture at all.

"Sorry, right, yes, please," Zander added, but Savannah had already retreated into the kitchen.

She fixed the drinks, Cade's neat, hers with two cubes of ice and Zander's with lots of Coke, and strained to hear the men through the open window. Either they were not speaking at all or they were saying something that neither wanted her to hear. She handed them their drinks while Cade hopped up and grabbed a kitchen chair. Apparently he was staying to make the conversation a three-some.

"So, what's on your mind tonight?" Savannah asked Zander. Cade had arranged her chair closer to him, she noticed.

"Well, I'm really just stopping by because I was driving by. I didn't know about this last night or even this morning when we talked. An importer is flying into San Fran late and called from New York this morning to let us know. He wants to meet tomorrow and taste some wines, but I've got to have them to his hotel, since he has several wine makers to meet."

"That's great news!" Savannah said with real interest. Cade stared straight ahead and sipped, he could care less.

"Yeah, it really is. Mother is over the moon about this opportunity. So-you can just imagine her- she spent the afternoon selecting wines with me, calling down to get a hotel suite and food ordered-just everything. I'm going tonight to get it set up and let the wines rest and then he's supposed to meet with me by late morning tomorrow."

"I can't wait to hear how it goes!"

Zander drained his whiskey and Coke. "Yeah, me, too! Hey, I really need to get going, but I'll plan on seeing you Thursday night." Zander stood, preparing to leave, then, boldly turning to Cade, he asked: "Would you mind giving us a minute alone?"

Cade's eyes narrowed. "It's my porch and I don't remember asking you here."

Zander threw up his hands. "Champion, I just stopped by for a few-"

"Stop it!" Savannah hissed. Turning to Cade, she implored him with her eyes, as if to say 'if you give us a minute, he'll leave'.

Cade sighed heavily, feeling a sadness so thick he almost choked. "I'm gonna check the stock." Turning to Zander, his eyes were hard. "I don't expect to see you when I get back."

———————— •◆• ————————

"Damn it, Savannah! It's only a couple weeks 'til the sale and you're blowing this hair out like you *want* these Herefords to have curls!" Cade exclaimed as he ran his hand over the calf's ribs in a vain attempt to straighten her hair. It was blown into a whirl rather than up and straight the way they wanted it.

"What are you talking about?" Savannah turned away from the calf she was working on and yelled over the noise of the fans and the blower.

"This, damn it!" Cade hollered again, jabbing an index finger into the ribs of the unsuspecting heifer. She pinned her ears back and shied away in response.

Savannah kicked the blower off with the stomp of her boot against the switches. "Cade, I just hadn't gotten to her yet to fix that. One of the boys worked on her and he is still figuring out that blowing Hereford hair isn't like working on a Maine or a Shorthorn-"

"Well, you should have caught it before he got her this dry!" Cade yelled, taking an exasperated brush of the heifer's hair with his metal scotch comb.

Savannah had had enough for the day. She'd been trying, really trying, to be supportive of Cade's obvious frustration at being hurt, the pressure at having to put together a new facility, hire new help, and get sale stock ready all at the same time, but his attitude toward her –the person helping him- was B.S.! It was the third thing he had yelled at her about and it wasn't even lunchtime. First, she hadn't mixed feed right (he had decided to change the ration but informed no one). Second, he thought she left a comb tine-side-up in the wash rack (*she* hadn't, but took the heat for it), and now hair she would have fixed if he had shown up five minutes later he was bitching about.

"Really? *Really,* Cade? I'm out here busting my ass for you when I should be working on my book and you're yelling at me *again*?"

"What do you mean again?" Cade acted oblivious, a move that pissed Savannah off even more.

Swinging around to face him, she shoved the comb in her pocket and hung her jug of spray sheen by the handle on the gate. "I'm done with you for the day, Cade," she said angrily and stormed out of the barn.

Cade was slower than usual as he ran after her, the effort at half-running creating a burning sensation in his ribs and back. "Get back here, there's no reason to run off like that!"

Wrong thing to say…

Savannah spun around so fast that she flung dirt and rocks and almost knocked herself off balance. She braced both hands on her hips and readied for the fight. "I cannot believe the nerve you have, Cade Champion! You are a Class- A asshole sometimes! You know that?" she shouted as Cade caught up, breathing hard.

"Oh wait, you don't know that, apparently, because if you did you wouldn't ask me WHY I am mad!"

Cade leaned forward, hands on his knees, sucking air. "Well, why are you mad?"

"*Seriously*?" Savannah was incredulous. "You are treating me like the help! The FFA boys are now scared to talk to you since you're being such a jerk and you're yelling at me for being your laborer and your intermediary?"

"Yeah, I mean, so what if I got a little pissy with you about some sloppy work, but hey, I guess, you are the help!" Cade was yelling now, his breathing ragged.

The remark about sent Savannah into orbit. "What!???"

"Yeah, I mean its not like we have anything else between us, right? Ya know, last night I jokingly called us an old married couple, but that's not quite right, is it, Savannah? Nope, I feel old all right, like your old helpless dad sitting on the porch after you get my dinner and then you run off with your boyfriend. It's about to make me sick!"

"Cade that is no excuse to act like a jerk to me about the barn!"

Cade shook his head in mock agreement. "You're right its not, but that ass-wipe shows up at my house then asks me to leave so he can be alone with you. Did you enjoy a hot makeout session while I went to check cows? Did you enjoy letting him put his hand-"

"Cade! That is not fair and you know it!" Savannah was livid now.

"You're God damned right it's not fair!" Cade roared, his voice hoarse with emotion. "I've got you living under my roof, we have a great time and great conversation during the day, but I can't touch you! No! Zander shows up and he gets what I want!"

Savannah started to choke back sobs, but she didn't know why. "Cade, I don't know what I want. It's just not that simple-"

Cade shook his head and averted his eyes, his temper now gone. "I'm sorry I've treated you rudely today and I'm sorry I yelled. I shouldn't do that. But, I'm not sure if I can keep this up-us sleeping 10 feet apart and still 10,000 miles away."

Savannah tried to think of something to say, but couldn't. Cade turned and walked away.

———————————— • ◆ • ————————————

Later, Savannah sat alone on the cottage porch. She and Cade hadn't talked much since the fight earlier. He told her he didn't need help with chores. She told him she was going to drive into town and write for a while at the coffee shop. When she returned at dark, he was in his bedroom with the door shut. She considered calling Zander, but she really didn't want him. Besides that would just endorse Cade's point if she ran off tonight, so deciding to check on things at home, she dialed Eddie.

"Hey there, Savvy! How's things in sunny California?" Eddie asked. He was so cheerful these days Savannah hardly recognized him.

"Well, it's not real sunny, actually. Cade and I go from getting along to fighting and its starting to cool off here," she remarked and tightened the jacket around her neck. She even had on a pair of Cade's white cotton gloves. She certainly hadn't told Eddie she was staying at Cade's cottage, but he knew about the fact that they were working on a ranch together.

"Well, I got nothing for the two a you, that's for sure," Eddie commented. "I'm not a real expert at romance, you know."

Savannah laughed and so did Eddie. "Well, how is Crystal? That still going good?"

"Sure is. Going so well I figure I'll screw it up somehow anytime."

"Ah, don't say that, Eddie. She must really like you!"

"I hope so," Eddie said, then changing the subject, "You gonna be back before the North American?" Eddie asked, referencing the major livestock show held every November in Louisville, Kentucky.

"No, I guess I'll miss it this year," Savannah hadn't considered that she wouldn't be back until almost Thanksgiving, if she did indeed need until mid-November to finish the book. And, there was the Pedrocelli Ranch sale coming up…

"Well, the seasons are changing around here, for sure. I wanted to tell ya that I turned cows out on stalks the other day,"

"That's good. I'm glad we talked to the neighbor about using his field this summer. I love seeing cows on stalks. Did you get all the big round bales bought?"

"Yeah, sure did. Got 'em put away and I went ahead and spoke for about 30 more in case we have end up having a long winter. You know, you were a little short last April when it came down to it."

Savannah smiled. *Eddie taking responsibility and thinking ahead! What a concept.*

"You're right, we were. Thank you, Eddie.

"Yeah, we're good on about everything, except if you want to put in more embryos for next year, I still haven't found enough recipient cows for that."

"I just can't believe nobody around has cows they want to sell us for receips!"

"I know you want to do more of it, but you gotta understand, people around here aren't real innovative about using embryo transfer just yet."

"I suppose you're right. I guess I'll call Clint again and see if he has any better ideas."

Savannah hung up and stared into the dark thinking so much about home that she could almost hear the sound of cow's hooves crunching on frosty corn stalks and smell the dried leaves in the air. It wouldn't be long before she needed to go home and just be done with California. And Zander.

And yes, Cade.

TWELVE
UPPING THE GAME (S)

"What in the hell is that?" Cade yelled over the din of the fans as he started for the barn door. He had just handed Savannah her first beer and popped his.

It had been a few days since the fight. Cade had apologized and so had she, but they were both reeling from some of the truth of it. They had gone back to working and hanging out in the evening - a routine that seemed safe enough on the surface – Zander had not been back, a fact that also helped the two of them trying to repair the angry words. Over dinner on the porch, Cade had tried broach the question of 'was there a them' but Savannah just wasn't ready to go there and told him as much. She really didn't know what to do but to 'get through' finishing her book and thinking about getting home to clear her head. With Cade everything was emotionally charged all the time. Savannah supposed that was one reason why she kept it going with Zander; being with him was fun, simple, and different. It was also a distraction and it didn't require her to feel like she was loosing control of her wits every time he kissed her. It was just fine.

Savannah was as perplexed as Cade with the tremendous noise which sounded like a tornado or a train descending on the roof.

"Oh my God!" Savannah exclaimed as she and Cade watched a sleek black helicopter land right in the barnlot.

"You gotta be shitting me," Cade growled as Zander emerged from the rig bearing flowers and an enormous box.

Savannah's hands flew to her mouth in shock.

Zander was grinning from ear to ear and dressed in a skin-tight pair of black pants and an equally fitted blazer. His burgundy tie was tied in a huge knot, NFL-commentator style.

"I realized that I haven't treated you to an evening out in San Francisco! So, I called a restauranteur friend of mine and he's arranged a private dinner on his rooftop terrace. Since he has a helipad, I thought we'd just zoom over there in this!" he said proudly gesturing toward the helicopter.

"Zander! Wow! A *helicopter*," Savannah could hardly contain her excitement - or embarrassment. She did not dare glance at Cade. "Well, I have nothing to wear! I can't go like this! I'm in dirty jeans."

"Not to worry, I thought of that, too. Look inside."

Savannah accepted the box wrapped in a flurry of logo ribbon from Adelle's the fancy boutique in St. Helena that Francie had recommended to Macy. Inside a darling bright red sleeveless dress, white cardigan, and a pair of heeled sandals were nestled in pink tissue paper.

"Zander-how-"

"His mother, I'd guess," Cade remarked caustically. "Although, maybe you do shop at a chick store, Zander, come to think of it."

"If that is slander against my brother because he is gay, then you're a real piece of work, Champion," Zander shot back.

Cade didn't miss a beat. "Nope. Actually, I meant you. Did you get those skinny jeans you're wearing there? Don't bother bringing me a pair-I doubt they have men's sizes-"

"If you'd like to ask Savannah if she considers me a man you could do that-she would know-"

"That is ENOUGH!" Savannah was disgusted. "I'll tell Francie myself that I appreciate the outfit and since it looks like it will fit, I'm going to change and we're going to go."

Savannah marched off to the bathroom, leaving the two men to circle each other like dogs in a pack. Zander looked smug. Cade looked as though he was going to commit murder.

———————— • ◆ • ————————

Later it wasn't lost on Cade that Zander had chosen to have the helicopter pick Savannah up at the ranch instead of waiting until she returned to Kinsley's. Cade knew she was close to leaving and that the fight they had was pushing her away. Zander had intentionally meant to demonstrate his wealth and he had literally landed in Cade's world and taken Savannah out of it; the message was clear; he was serious about Savannah.

Zander was upping his game. Cade didn't think Savannah realized how serious Zander actually was. He knew in his bones that she was just being with him for a lark, even if she refused to admit it. But that thought didn't stop his blood from boiling.

They would have close moments, moments where his heart would soar and he would swear she warmed to him, but then, just as quick, she would push away – or Zander would conveniently swoop in and interrupt before he could secure a foothold. Still, Cade could feel that Savannah cared for him, too, but the wound between them was deep and she flat refused to let him repair the chasm. Besides, she was plain stubborn.

"Private terrace in *San-Fran*," Cade muttered aloud. He sulked alone on his porch, sipping his third bourbon. "It's time to show that prick what I've got."

He would need a better plan to win her back. Just telling her what to do and who to do it with wouldn't work. The good thing was, he knew that and Zander didn't. He needed something more though, something to trigger her deepest affections, something to tie her to him so he wouldn't automatically lose her when she went home.

"What do I have that Zander could never give her?" Cade said aloud to the group of show heifers bedded down in the traps. He had refilled his glass and walked out to check stock.

"You girls must thing I'm nuts - a lonely man talking with you at night. Savannah wouldn't, she loves her cows-"

Suddenly, the proverbial light bulb went off and Cade jumped with enthusiasm. The heifers scattered a few paces and looked back at him curiously.

"Yes! Savannah loves her cows-that's it!"

Cade flipped open his phone and dialed Clint Cascade.

"Hey, Man! How the hell you been?" Cade began as they exchanged greetings.

"Yeah, yeah, I know, its close to the sale, that's for sure. Hey, I gotta a deal I wanna run past you."

He had a plan to become a permanent fixture in Savannah's life and the perfect way to partner with Clint that would automatically make him partners with Savannah, too.

———————— •❖• ————————

"You *cannot* be serious," Savannah whispered aloud as she went to the bedroom window. "Oh Dear Lord, Cade is going to freak out."

The Pedrocelli guest cottage's storage room that had become her bedroom was on the second floor. A lovely antique vanity that had evidently been left behind by some previous resident was her only piece of furniture besides the bed, but Savannah had taken to using it to get ready-it was far more private than trying to navigate Cade in the cottage's one bathroom, with a door that barely shut. At the sound of a vehicle, Savannah went to the window, correctly assuming that Zander was early; she could not have dreamed he would arrive in a sleek gunmetal grey Rolls Royce complete with a driver.

That Zander – *and* Francie - had invited her to a fancy charity benefit in San Francisco Cade was aware. She justified attending it to him saying that since Francie had asked her to go she couldn't just say no to an offer like that just because he was irritated about 'the Zander situation'. Francie had even sent over a personal shopper from Adelle's with dresses for Savannah to try on. When Savannah saw the price tags -several of them well over $1,000 - she called Francie to let her know she simply could not afford it. But, Francie reassured her; the dresses were only meant to be rented and not to worry because Francie would be delighted to cover the cost. Savannah agreed, reluctantly at first, but now, as she admired herself in the floor-length turquoise dress and strappy silver heels, she had to admit-she was excited about playing dress up.

Savannah cracked the window so she could hear the men conversing. They didn't sound to be arguing, but the tones weren't conversational either. She planned to spend a bit more time on her cosmetics and add a few more pins to the up-do she had attempted, but leaving Cade and Zander alone was not a good plan.

When Savannah emerged onto the front porch, the reaction was what she had hoped for – Cade looked at her appreciatively and without considering Zander, he rose and walked to her. "Savannah, wow. You are stunning," he said, then breathing into her ear he added "I hope you wish it was me taking you out." He gently laid a kiss on her cheek.

Savannah didn't have time to consider her answer.

"Hey! Enough of that!" Zander remarked as he stepped in closer. "tu es belle, Savannah, as the French would say, you are beautiful."

Savannah batted her eyes slightly like a coquette. "Thank you."

"And, as the French would do, I have brought you something to compliment this beautiful outfit," Zander said as he pulled a small red box bearing the words *Cartier* from his jacket pocket. "Please open it."

Savannah's eyes darted to Cade. "Oh, Zander, thank you for the gift, but let's get going and I'll open it in the car-"

"No Savannah, open it now, I want to put it on you."

Zander acted smug, she suspected the gift would be expensive and his overt show of money in front of Cade was making Savannah's stomach turn. The fun of playing dress up had just turned sour.

———————— • ◆ • ————————

The cottage was completely dark when Savannah and Zander returned. If it hadn't been for the buzzing security light in the driveway, Savannah would have tripped up the porch steps as Zander's Rolls slinked elegantly out of the driveway.

Not like I expected him to be waiting up with the porch light on, I guess, Savannah mused. She knew Cade had probably been furious and was sulking.

Speaking of sulking, she and Zander had had a really wonderful evening until Zander decided to start a fight by telling the driver to take them to Napa. She had to yell at the driver to turn around and take her to Sonoma. As Savannah felt around for the porch railing, she started to feel everything unraveling. California was starting to feel very crowded.

Savannah decided against turning on the kitchen light, it was only a few dim steps to the cottage's stairs and there was no reason to risk an argument with Cade, too. Savannah fumbled around silently, slipping off her heels by the back door and sliding them into a corner, then laying aside her purse and shawl. She stepped to the sink and began to fill a glass of water as quietly as she could. Suddenly, she felt rather than heard a presence behind her and that presence was wrapping ironclad arms around her waist and pressing warm lips to her neck.

"Savannah, I'm so glad you're back," Cade murmured against her neck. Cade's breath was laced with whiskey. "You need to come to me now," he said huskily. Savannah started to push him back, but his mouth found hers as he pushed her against the sink.

Savannah tried to scramble away, but Cade's weight pinned her in place. His hands were in her hair, tearing down the up-do, grasping almost wildly at the strands as hairpins sprung away and made soft 'pings' as they hit the floor. Savannah had thought with Cade's broken ribs that there was a measure of safeness about being there, that he wouldn't 'bother her'. But, she had been wrong. Cade was there and he felt strong.

"You cannot be with him, its time to go to bed with me," Cade was saying against her mouth. Savannah found herself giving into the kiss, her hands found his cheeks.

Maybe in the morning he won't remember that I kissed him back…

Suddenly, Cade jerked, rather, *stumbled*, back, taking her with him as he careened into the small kitchen table sending a chair crashing. Savannah regained her posture and reached out to help him right himself. "Cade, your ribs! You need to go lie down-"

Cade nodded his head groggily and reached for her as she attempted to lift the 240-pound man. "Yeah, uh, that hurt a little, but don't worry, Sa-vaaa-naaah," Cade's words were oddly slurred. "There's other parts of me that work really good." Cade attempted to put his hand on his crotch.

"Cade, you're drunk. Go lay down and go to sleep." She helped him up, bracing him partly against the wall and doorframe, party against herself. She clicked on the hallway light as Cade leaned on her, causing her to support nearly his entire weight.

How much did he drink?

"I'm drunk, yeah, oh yeah, but I'm thinking maybe those pills started to work, huh, Baby?" Cade stumbled back, knocking over another chair, then he slumped against the wall again, this time banging his head. He evidently didn't feel it.

"Oh, Cade, you took some pain meds, too?" Savannah was concerned. That explained his complete lack of coordination. There was only one way to get Cade to lie down and that was to fool him. Savannah reached out to Cade. "Okay, you win, I'll come to bed with you." Cade's lips circled upward in a crooked leering grin. "Lean against me, okay?"

Cade did as he was told and Savannah half drug him the few feet to the bedroom. "Okay, you first, " Savannah mumbled as she sort of aimed Cade over the center of his bed. "Lie down now."

As soon as she let go, Cade collapsed into a heap on the bed. She realized he was fully dressed, dirty boots and all. Savannah hovered over him for a moment deciding what to do. Cade's eyes were already closed, but he was talking gibberish. She knelt closer. "Shhh."

Then, in sudden burst of delirious energy Cade reached out for her, pulling her onto the bed, half on him, half beside him. "Mmmmnn, that's better," Cade mumbled. "Just stay."

Savannah rolled to his right side and laid her head on his chest. She shoved a pillow under his head and adjusted his arms, one around her back and one across his torso. He was snoring instantly.

Savannah, clad in her beautiful thousand-dollar rental, let herself fall asleep next to a drunken, pain-med-stoned Cade Champion in a little cottage on a ranch in California.

———— •◆• ————

"Hey," Cade said gently as he peeked his head into her open bedroom doorway. "I bet I owe you one hell of an apology."

Savannah looked up at him and placed her hands on her hips in mock irritation. She wondered what he actually remembered. "How's your head?"

"Ugg, not good. You beat me with a bat or what?"

"No, actually, I was nice and tucked you in, if you didn't notice."

"I did and somebody took of my clothes - unless I did that-"

"Nope, that was me, too. After you wacked your head against the wall twice, I figured you could use a little help getting to bed," Savannah said, laughing lightly.

Cade touched the back of his head. "That explains the throbbing –well- that and the whiskey," Cade grimaced and then turning more serious, he said, "I know I came onto you last night. I don't really know what I did exactly, but it probably wasn't gentlemanly. I'm sorry."

So he did remember their kiss…

"Cade, I'd say it's okay, but actually, its not! We cannot live under the same roof, we have to admit that!"

"Don't say that."

"Well, it doesn't matter, really, because I need to leave anyway, mother is coming over for a few days and I am not having her catch me here."

"What do you mean? Are you packing?" Cade's head hurt, he didn't want her to leave *today*.

"Savannah, I'm sorry for last night. If you're leaving today because of that, if I was weird, or scared you, I didn't mean to. But, for the last couple of weeks its like we get close and then you slip away," Cade ran his hands through his hair and sat down on her bed. "I wish I could say it wasn't but, it's about killing me."

"Cade, I'm sorry. I'll come back over to the ranch, but I've got plans and-"

"He doesn't know you at all, Savannah. All the fancy stuff in the world can't buy your love. We both know it."

"You're right about that-we actually had a fight on the way home, so you'll be glad to know the evening wasn't that great."

"Then dump him and let's be together!"

"No."

Cade felt his exasperation with Savannah rising. He slammed his palms sharply against his knees. "Savannah, if it wasn't *you* he wanted, I'd actually feel sorry for that boy. I don't think you realize how serious he actually is about you."

That thought struck Savannah by surprise. "I know he likes me and is attracted to me, but he could have any rich little winery girl he wants and we don't really have anything in common so-"

"Exactly! So cut this charade with him!"

Savannah shot him a look and proceeded to zip her suitcase.

Cade tried a different approach. "You're being cruel Savannah! You know that? You're actually being mean to Zander, using him only to drive a wedge - a fake wedge - between the two of us. He's just an excuse!"

"Well maybe he is!" Savannah shot back, surprising herself that she admitted it. "You know, but it's just easier and there is no pressure to have-"

"To have what?"

"To have all these feelings that I don't know what to do with, Cade!"

"Its called love Savannah," he said, his eyes growing round as he moved to embrace her. "Come here. Please-"

"I can't, Cade! I don't know what I want!" Savannah turned and dashed down the stairs.

THIRTEEN

THE WINE TASTING

"Zander, honey, you are being such a peach!" Francie said sweetly as Zander kissed his mother's cheek and then, standing, he bent to put a much sexier smooch on Savannah's lips. She blushed and smiled, but she didn't really want the PDA.

"Today is all about you three beautiful women and between Xave and I we're going to make sure we show you a fabulous time! I'm just going to order us a bottle of bubbles and we'll enjoy that and map out our day," he added, heading into the winery.

"Francie, this is just gorgeous. And, your son, well, he is totally adorable!" Jessica Morgan mewed as she leaned back and let the warm morning sun touch the points of her lovely face. Watching her mother, Savannah thought she was the most beautiful and elegant woman in the world. Jessica had arrived at noon the day before, they'd already had a grand time, enjoying dinner and a vineyard tour of Kingsley Estate the evening before and staying up half the night talking together in the guest cottage. Savannah had told her mother about Zander, but definitely *not* about Cade. Today was going to be a marvelous day of tasting in Napa, complete with the limo that Zander had ordered to drive them around. Savannah was in as good a mood as she'd been in months. It was so much fun to be spoiled.

"Jessica, we're simply delighted to host you and Savannah!" Francie exclaimed as she adjusted her enormous sunglasses. "I don't think it will be too warm today," she mused, reaching for the sample of chardonnay that everyone had been served as a welcome wine.

"It's really a treat to get such an insider's view of the Napa wine country, I really appreciate that you've set up such a fun day," Jessica was saying.

Francie waved her hands as if her efforts were nothing special. "Actually, I'm just old news in the valley these days. Really, it's the boys that have all the connections. Wait until we get to the new winery that Xave's friend just opened. Dear Lord, its gaudy, but I have to admit that I'm dying to see it. It's actually a castle that's been years in the-"

"Oh my God," Savannah whispered. Her eyes travelled out across the front entrance to the winery and into the parking lot where, emerging from an F-350 diesel farm truck was Cade, following by Monica and even Hollis.

Francie grimaced only for a moment as she saw the trio. Calmly, she swirled and sipped the Chardonnay, then turned up her nose, leaned over and spat in the bucket. "Jessica, you're about to meet my precocious little sister and her ruff-neck husband. And, the tall dangerously good looking thing with them is their new show cattle manager, Cade Champion."

In spite of herself, Savannah sucked in a loud breath.

"I believe your daughter knows him," Francie remarked.

Savannah gulped the chardonnay.

Jessica's brow arched pleasantly as a nod to Francie and she turned to her daughter. "Cade Champion? Is that YOUR Cade Champion, the one who broke your heart in Denver?" she whispered.

Savannah was fixated on the sight of Cade sauntering toward her, his eyes never leaving her face. "Yes," she managed to eek out. She grabbed Jessica's chardonnay and gulped it, too.

"This day is about to get interesting," Jessica muttered just as Cade reached the group, striding over the little decorative fence around the tasting patio that was meant to indicate that guests should check in at the front door and be *invited* to sit. He paid no attention to the 'Club Member's Only' sign.

Cade approached Jessica and bowed deeply, his grin as broad as Savannah had ever seen it. "You are sure beautiful, Ma'am, so I can only guess you must be Savannah's mother, Jessica, that I've heard so much about."

Jessica turned on her considerable charm, smiling sweetly and extending her hand. "I am, and I suppose you are the Cade Champion that I have heard so much about."

Cade clasped Jessica's hand as if to shake then turned over her palm and kissed it. Jessica beamed. Savannah rolled her eyes.

Cade grinned and turned to Francie. "Francie, you are so pretty today, as always," he uttered as he kissed her hand as well. Francie giggled in spite of herself. Savannah rolled her eyes again. Finally, he came around the table, bent down and kissed her cheek. Savannah blushed profusely and turned away as Cade whispered: "I cannot believe you forgot to invite me to this little wine party."

"Champion, what in the hell are you doing here?" Zander's voice was tight and angry. He was bearing a bottle of sparking wine and four glasses.

Cade laid his hand lightly on Savannah's shoulder as he rose to his full height. He laughed cockily, as if he were completely oblivious to that fact that he had upended the entire day's plan. "Hey, there, Zander! I heard there was a wine tasting trip today and thought I'd enjoy seeing Napa," Cade's hand lightly stroked Savannah's shoulder. He watched Zander's eyes watch him do it with sheer delight. "Ya know, I haven't had a chance to take in the local sites since I've been so busy with the sale," Cade stepped forward and stunned Zander by removing the bottle from his hands. "Buddy, we're gonna need a couple more glasses. Would you mind grabbing them?"

Jessica laughed out loud-an utterly unladylike full belly laugh. She watched her daughter and Cade, then met his eyes. No wonder her daughter had been completely smitten by Cade Champion.

"I was wrong, Savannah. Honey, this day just got really, really damned interesting."

———— •◆• ————

The second fiasco of the day was figuring out how everyone *not* invited on the wine tasting trip was going to ride along. Of course the limo had plenty of room, but Zander threw a fit when Cade took the liberty of climbing right into the vehicle without as much as a question. Francie was not overly pleased either, but wasn't going to allow Zander to look ungracious, so she encouraged everyone to pile in for the day. Still, a small argument ensued between Francie and Zander outside the limo, making him the last person to board. Cade had conveniently seated himself next to Savannah, with Jessica on Savannah's other side. Zander was livid as he slumped in next to his Uncle Hollis.

"Cade, what on earth have you done?" Savannah muttered.

Cade reached his arm behind the seat and extended his long legs, making himself comfortable. "Well, Monica mentioned to me yesterday afternoon that with your mom visiting Francie was taking you all wine tasting today. So, I told her, 'hey, I'm gonna take the day off today'. Well, you know her, she says 'oh, I'm going with you then' and I'm thinking, I am not letting *you* get the wrong idea," he squeezed Savannah's shoulder. "So, this morning I told Hollis that Monica wanted to take me wine tasting today and I asked if he would mind coming along."

Cade always seemed to have a game. "I'm certain he didn't want her running off with you all day so he grudgingly agreed."

Cade shrugged. "I guess, but at least he agreed to drive!" Then, raising his voice, he called out to Zander. "Surely you've got cocktails in here! Let's pop another top!"

Zander was sulking, but reached into the built-in wine cellar. "Booze is the only thing that is going to get us through this day."

———————————•◆•———————————

"Some of the finest pedigreed cabernets in the world come from our vineyards," the wine steward was saying as he and an aide poured each guest six different Cabernets into six enormous Reidel glasses. When Zander set up a wine tasting day, he certainly went all out. They were already at their third winery, this one a massive brick structure with bold oak beams and thick red velvet drapery everywhere.

"Looks like a whorehouse," Cade quipped as he passed by Zander and Savannah. He'd taken to sitting with Jessica so he'd have *someone* to talk with. Zander had absurdly kept Savannah as far away from him as possible since the first stop and Monica, with both Hollis and Francie along, had been thankfully well behaved. Besides, after their first glass of wine, she and Francie had found something to argue about at every stop. Hollis stayed in the limo to nap.

As soon as they arrived, the group was escorted to the cellar, Savannah was seated in between Zander and Francie, but Cade had taken a set directly across from her, making not looking at him impossible as their host droned on.

"As you approach the first wine, you'll notice the little nuances of color – the intricate shades of garnet and vermillion - then on the nose, the bouquet hints at spices, like cardamom and even anise-" suddenly the server observed Cade taking a drink of his wine and he waved a finger at him, looking offended. "Sir. Sir!" he raised his voice for emphasis. "I wasn't through describing the wines-"

"Well don't let me hold you up!" Cade remarked with a wink at Savannah as he enjoyed a sip.

The wine steward looked appalled that Cade had not waited until he finished his diatribe to indulge.

"You'll have to excuse him, Alonzo," Zander said. "Not everyone understands the appropriate way to appreciate wine at a private tasting."

Savannah was stunned at Zander's snobbery. "Zander, that was rude!"

"Well, hey, its just true," Zander sniffed. "Are you chilly, Babe, here, take my blazer."

"Actually, I've tasted wine all over this valley, Alonzo, and if your guests are ready to enjoy the wine, I believe they should not be chastised!" Francie said, nodding at Cade and taking a healthy swig. Then, having swirled it, she spat in provided bucket. "Honestly, this one seems a bit off."

Cade grinned and raised a glass. "Cheers!"

Savannah giggled, sniffing a little wine up her nose.

Alonzo was highly displeased at being berated by none other than Francine Kingsley and having lost control of his tasting.

"Well, uh – certainly - yes, do enjoy at your own pace," he picked up the second glass. "Now then, this wine is one of our champions. Delicious now, but its age worthy having won three gold metals at the San Francisco-"

"Well, that's my name!" Cade announced.

"Pardon me, Sir?" Alonzo turned to Cade, his patience thin.

"Yep, my name is Champion. Cade Champion and don't you forget it, right Savannah?"

Savannah didn't mean to laugh, and certainly didn't mean to let forth the little hiccup, but it was their third winery…

"Did you just burp?" Cade laughed aloud, arching one of his full brows at her in mock disgust. "You're an awfully pretty girl to burp at the table, Young Lady."

"No! That was more like a hiccup, I think," Savannah giggled, hiccupping yet again.

"I don't understand-" Alonzo looked as though he could spit nails.

"His name is Champion, that's his last name," Jessica commented. She was a little appalled that Cade and Savannah were quite obviously flirting across the table in front of everyone.

"Oh, and he's proud of it, aren't you?" Savannah quipped, raising her glass. "To The Great Cade Champion!"

Cade stood, as if preparing to offer remarks and bowed deeply. "It's about time you acknowledged me as great, Savannah!"

Savannah laughed even harder as Monica rose her glass. If she couldn't have the cowboy to herself, at least it was fun pissing off Francie and her nephew, she thought.

"To Cade!" announced Monica.

Jessica joined. "To Cade!"

Alonzo meekly raised his glass.

Zander was livid.

———————•◆•———————

"Finally lunch!" Cade remarked as he group stumbled out of the limo and up to the front gates of Sterling Winery and Vineyards.

"Yes, Xave and I have arranged a rooftop picnic for us. This will be quite fun for our tourists since we get to take a gondola ride up," Zander said smugly. "I'll just go check in and see how that is coming along," he stepped away as the group meandered around gazing at the knick-knacks and wine bottle displays in the winery's lobby. Cade wandered outside in search of some fresh air. Savannah watched him go. With Zander busy, she wanted to follow Cade even though her better judgment tried to intervene. "I'm headed to the restroom," she said to her mother as she took leave of the group. Jessica watched Savannah saunter away knowing full well the restroom wasn't outside.

"Having fun?" she said to Cade. He was leaning on his elbows over a railing, absently rubbing one bicep, revealing a large purple bruise.

"What happened here?" Without thinking she stepped closer and touched it lightly.

"Oh, I used my body as a human fence the other day with one the mama cows and I got backed into a post," Cade said flippantly. "Old rip stepped on me, too."

"You need to be more careful, Cade. I've only been gone a couple of days! Your ribs aren't even healed and now you're gonna hurt something else," she admonished.

Cade's eyes scanned her face noticing the way her cheeks were lightly burnished by the sun and flushed from all the morning's wine.

She is so damned beautiful.

He ached to hold her, to take her away. It was about all he could do to physically stand the sight of Zander mauling her with his skinny little fingers.

"You need to be careful standing this close to me, Young Lady. I might just kiss you."

"Oh, Cade, not that again," Savannah feigned irritation but she was flirting and she knew it.

Cade shook his head and feathered back his golden brown hair.

She just might be the death of me.

Spotting the gondolas he had a better idea. "Come on!" he grabbed her forearm and Savannah, knocked slightly off balance, trailed after him.

"Where are we going?"

"To take a gondola ride!"

Laughing like two teenagers, they piled into the gondola just as the rest of the group was coming out of the tasting room.

"That bastard!" Zander grumbled as she and Cade lifted off.

"This ride up is amazing!" Savannah gushed as she stood, peering out over the valley as the gondola swayed slightly on its ascent.

"Yeah, pretty damn cool way to go drink wine," Cade acknowledged. "It's also a very romantic moment. I think we should definitely mark this with a nice slow kiss," he added as he slipped his arm around Savannah's waist.

Savannah lurched away, a move that set the gondola to swaying roughly. She stumbled to the bench. Cade sighed and plopped onto the bench opposite her.

"Better not do that again!" she said, gripping the sides.

"What? You try to tip this thing over or me try kiss you?"

"Kiss me! I wouldn't have jumped if you hadn't!" Savannah's world was swimming a bit.

Cade studied Savannah for a long moment to the point that she grew irritated.

"What?"

"I'm just sitting here wondering when you are going to come off your high horse and just admit you want me as bad as I want you."

Cade had some nerve!

"What is that supposed to mean?"

"It means what I said. Come on, would you mind so awfully much if I did kiss you?"

Savannah had to smile at his persistence. "No, I suppose I would not. I mean, we were pretty attracted to each other when we met."

Cade nodded in agreement. "And we still are and you know it."

"I can agree that I'd like it if you kissed me, but we just can't. I'm dating Zander." Savannah hoped she sounded convincing.

Cade rolled his eyes. "I am just about done putting up with that. Admit that you are done with him and let's be together. You're leading that poor boy on and you know that, too."

Savannah gazed out the window. The gondola was nearing the top of the mountain. It was true, she was about over the fun with Zander. He had become more of a friend with a lot of fun money and perks, but her attraction to him had waned.

———————— • ◆ • ————————

The rooftop picnic proved worth the ride up with the view of the valley below through the redwoods stunning and the meal of grilled tri-tip, salads, and dessert, with ever flowing wines all buzz-worthy and delicious. Everyone was in a boozy but happy mood as they organized to descend; everyone except Zander who had grown moody and possessive. He insisted that Savannah ride with him alone on the gondola and she did so without argument. Zander set to kissing her the moment the door shut, getting aggressive, pressing into Savannah so heavily that the metal frame of the gondola window gouged her back.

"Easy, Zander. You're hurting me." Savannah pushed him away.

Zander didn't let up. "Come on, you've been flirting with that redneck all day. It's time you and I had a little more fun-" his hand reached under the skirt and began crawling along her thigh.

"Zander! Don't!"

"What? You'd rather be in here making out with your Cowboy?"

A flicker of guilt shaded her face.

"Zander, come on. Don't be like that. We're all having a fun day-"

"Not really," was all he said.

———————◆·———————

"Your last stop of the day is going to be the absolute most *dee-vine*!" gushed Xave as he flung open the limo door.

"Oh my Gosh!" Savannah breathed. They had indeed driven up to a castle, just as Francie had described. Though the area had been made to look medieval, complete with a moat and draw bridge, the monstrosity stuck out ridiculously among the Napa Valley foothills.

"Come on! Get out everyone, I have canapés and *sooo* much wine!" Xave announced excitedly as everyone disembarked and took in the castle's massive entry hall. "Sorry Ian can't be with us today - he sends lots of love, of course! But, Google or some company like that called him into a meeting in SanFran, so – well -you know!"

Cade hung back, letting everyone move into the building as Xave gushed on about the castle and his boyfriend's wealth. He watched Savannah on Zander's arm. She didn't look comfortable and Zander looked sullen. He could tell they were fighting and hoped he was the cause. Still, it grieved him to see her unhappy.

"Just how much *do* you love my daughter, Cade Champion?" came the sound of Jessica's firm, but silky voice over his left shoulder. Cade had stepped into an alcove with his glass of wine and slunk onto a couch. He was starting to get a headache.

"Is it that obvious?"

"To everyone, I'm afraid, " she said pointedly, seating herself beside him.

Cade sighed. "Jessica, I love her so much it hurts and I never stopped. I know she must have said I was a real asshole – and I was- but we both hurt each other so bad after Denver. I just wish I could fix it!"

Cade leaned back, exasperated. "I'm not sure what else to do to get her to trust me."

Jessica sipped her wine. She felt bad for the handsome man so smitten with her daughter. "Morgan women aren't known for our trust in men and that's probably my fault. But I know Savannah. She'll come around. Don't give up now."

———————— • ◆ • ————————

"Is that everyone? Gather around!" Xave demanded. Then not seeing Cade, he hollered: "Wait a sec-where's the New Cowboy? I heard he crashed the party? Monica, where's that sexy cowboy you hired?"

"Not sure. He hasn't been giving me the time of day," Monica remarked dryly not caring if anyone heard. Hollis was snoring in the limo.

Xave laughed hysterically. "Or me! All the hot one's are always sooo straight!" he nodded at Cade, who had emerged from the restroom. "Pity!"

A tour of the castle ensued with a new wine set up in every room. Finally, with everyone duly plied with vino, the group emerged on a balcony overlooking the vineyards and the moat. "And now, a tour of the bio-dynamic vineyards!" Xave announced. "We'll descend these stairs and ride out in a couple of these souped-up golf carts.

"Hey, I gotta take this call," Zander said to Savannah as they reached the bottom and everyone was settling into carts. "Take the tour-you'll like it," Zander was already on the phone. He grabbed a golf cart and drove off in the opposite direction.

"Ass! That leaves us short of being able to fit everyone!" Xave was annoyed that his brother didn't value the tour he'd orchestrated. "Well, I'll just call for someone to bring us another-"

"Don't worry about it, Buddy," Cade said to Xave in a jolly tone. "Savannah and I will just follow the group on this 4-wheeler here!" Cade indicated to a dust covered ATV parked under a nearby tree.

Xave looked disgusted. "But, it's so *dirty!*"

"It'll work," Savannah turned to Cade. "You driving or me?"

Cade's day had just improved dramatically.

———————— •◆• ————————

"This tour would be boring as hell if it weren't for the company," Cade mumbled against her ear as they parked yet again, the third stop on the tour so far. The rest of group all filed out of the golf carts, carrying their glasses of Sauvignon Blanc and dutifully following the vineyard manager's lead. Cade's hand lightly tightened on Savannah's leg, as if to discourage her from getting up. "This pose is giving me a lot of ideas and I'm just going to say so."

But Savannah didn't make any move to follow, loath to leave the comfortable position on the 4-wheeler. The last half an hour had just about driven her to distraction and she was more than glad Zander wasn't there to see. Cade riding behind her had shifted her attraction for him right into overdrive. His hands alternated between sitting on his thighs, to resting on her thighs, to snuggly around her waist as she got a little frisky on the inclines. She rode in between his legs, his long lean thighs hugging her tightly. Cade had tucked her inappropriately close to him but she was past caring. His body was warm, solid, and all man. She knew he was trying to act casual, but he had to be going crazy. The heat on her lower back felt near blistering it was so hot the way Cade's abdomen was pressed against it.

"I know. I'm not sure I buy into all this biodynamic stuff," Savannah turned slightly to Cade.

The group had descended over a hill and disappeared from view.

Cade's lips grazed her cheek, his nose was in her hair, his palm gently squeezed her thigh, mid way up. "I don't think I'll ever forget what you smell like, Savannah," he murmured.

Savannah's breath caught in her throat. Resisting Cade was like telling a tornado to go away.

He pushed aside the long hair at the nape of her neck sending shivers down her spine while his breath warmed her earlobes. "Or how you taste."

Cade's mouth took its time covering the soft area between her collarbone and her neck. She felt the timbre of his moan rumble against her back. She realized she was squeezing his thigh.

"Cade, you need to stop," she said weakly. "We can't sit here like this…"

Cade knew she was right, but they needed to be alone. Releasing her, he slowly pulled her to standing. "Why don't we take a walk-and not that way," he said nodding in the direction of the wine tasting party.

A pathway through the vines led them around another small hillside and past a grove of sequoia. Hand in hand, they walked without talking. They'd been descending the hill for a few moments when Cade spotted an old shack or barn that appeared to be a field office for the vineyard manager.

"There," Cade said, quickening the pace.

A small crew was working nearby, but they attempted to sneak by unnoticed.

"My God, I need you to myself," Cade groaned against her neck as he tried the door and then pushed them into the room. They slammed into a wall, knocking a basket of maps and papers to the floor. Savannah fell against him, the passion and emotions of the day, or of the entire fall, or of the months that had passed since they had broken each other's hearts, gushing out of her as she let herself melt into Cade. His kiss was crushing, her urgency to kiss back desperate. His hands cupped her hips, her thighs were around his waist, he was lifting her, carrying her across the dimly lit room.

Their kiss deepened as Cade deposited Savannah on a little desk. He pushed closer, cupping her chin with both hands, stepping between her legs. Savannah moaned at the feel of him pressing against her, his tongue dove deeper into her mouth, tracing her front teeth, while hers met his. Absurd suctions noises that should have made her giggle didn't matter as Cade's firm hands drove into her hairline and pulled her head back farther, taking more and more of her breath as they kissed. Savannah yielded to Cade like she never had. She was starving, absolutely ravenous for all of Cade Champion. She wanted him, she was enjoying him, he wanted her. She wasn't stopping or denying anymore that she needed to feel him again.

"Cade, you, I-" she had no idea what she was saying. It didn't matter, their bodies were doing the talking, covering the long months apart. She grabbed at the front of his button down, her hand slipping inside, feeling his warm, broad chest.

"What do you think you're doing, Young Lady? Two can play at that game," Cade rasped, his right hand sliding down her collarbone and inside her v-neck top, pushing it and her bra strap off her left shoulder. Savannah kissed him harder. "Cade, I, oh my-I cannot-"

As she arched back deeper for Cade's lips to dip to her neck, her hand brushed something on the desk behind her-a set of crystal Reidel tasting glasses- and the move sent them shattering to the floor with a crash.

They jumped at the sound of the fragile little glasses breaking everywhere on the concrete.

"Hey! What the hell's going on in there!" came an angry voice on the other side of the locked door. Whomever had caught them sneaking in was attempting to pull it open.

"Oops! Cade laughed, pulling back and adjusting his jeans. "Come on!" He quickly flung open the window, tossed out the screen and pulled Savannah out with him. They both scurried down the hill toward the castle. Savannah kept swatting Cade's hand away, but she just couldn't stop giggling and her heart was racing so fast and so erratically that she was sure she was having a heart attack. They stumbled along, coming out to the end of a row of vines where they were nearly run over by Zander.

"What the hell is this?" Zander demanded.

Cade attempted to explain. "Sorry, Man, Savannah is such a little farmer, she and I got talking with a couple of the crew guys and just lost track of time," Cade said, throwing his hands up as if he was innocent.

"How convenient that you were there with her, Champion," Zander scoffed, eying the pair. Cade's shirt was untucked and Savannah's neck was speckled red with razor burn. "Savannah, I think you and I should leave now."

"Zander, don't be upset," she began, but stopped, feeling futile. Trying to explain away what she had been doing with Cade wasn't something she wanted to deal with.

Cade stood his ground as she took a seat on the golf cart. His eyes never left hers.

"Cade, I'll give you a call about the barn tomorrow, okay?" she said meekly, knowing it was flimsy and feeling as though she were choosing the wrong side in an argument.

Cade had never felt so empty as he watcher her go.

———————— •◆• ————————

Savannah flung herself on the bed. The world was swirling and the room's edges were fuzzy. She just needed to sleep. The whole day had been one big comedy-tragedy-fiasco of drunks with agendas. Zander had borrowed Xave's car and they had left the castle before the rest of the group even returned from the tour. She had made Zander mad, even more so because she didn't bother trying to make an excuse for being with Cade. He'd dropped her off and left. He had a right to be angry. He believed they were dating; she felt like they were more like friends. But what about Cade? She had been kissing him-wildly, deliciously kissing him-and what did that mean? She had no idea what the hell she was doing, but it was time she started to sort it out.

"I'm so glad you came out, Mom. I really had a great time with you!" Savannah said warmly as she hugged Jessica. The Kingsley's driver was waiting to take her to the airport and had already loaded her bags.

"Yes, it was so much fun! I loved Francie – but you just knew she and I would hit it off!"

Savannah smugly nodded her agreement.

"Of course, while I can tell you love Francie, too, you certainly haven't fallen in love with her son, have you?"

Savannah was taken aback but she shouldn't have been. Jessica was a lawyer had always cross-examined her with ease. "Mother!"

Jessica laughed lightly. "Oh come on, Savannah-you think I was the only one who saw how you and Cade Champion flirted shamelessly all day? And, suddenly we're on the vineyard tour and the two of you simply disappeared-"

Savannah blushed to her roots. "I told you – and everyone - Cade and I got talking farming with the vineyard manager and got separated from the group. Besides, I was flushed from all the wine we drank-you know alcohol can make me blotchy."

Jessica smiled in the way a mother would, placing her hand lightly on her daughter's arm.

"Savannah dear, I love you, but you are lying to yourself. You are madly in love with Cade Champion and that handsome, sweet, man is madly in love with you."

FOURTEEN
CADE AND SAVANNAH

"I'm really glad you could come over today-it's actually gonna be the perfect day for this drive," Cade said. They were in front of the showbarn where Cade had just finished feeding the sale heifers and turned out. He was hoisting a ruck sack onto the 4-wheeler's utility rack. A cooler was already loaded and when Savannah drove in he was rigging up tarp straps to hold everything in place. "Yeah, it's the perfect weather this afternoon and clear - that's what will make this really nice - it's a clear day," Cade said again.

She didn't know what would happen when she got there; if she'd thought Cade would reach for her and sweep her into his arms, he didn't. In fact, he barely looked at her. Savannah observed him with curiosity. He was actually acting *nervous*, something she had never before witnessed in Cade Champion. The tips of his dark ash blonde hair were still wet and she could smell the clean, zesty scent of his skin. He had just showered.

"So where are we going exactly? You've kind of kept this a mystery!" Savannah queried as she approached. It had been four days since the wine tasting – and passionate kissing. She had remained at the Kingsley's since working on the book project, or at least pretending to when she could control her mind long enough to commit any effort to writing. Things with Zander had been cool, which was admittedly fine with her. He had kept busy working and she didn't push to look him up. They'd eaten dinner with Francie and Xave the evening before, the first time she'd interacted with Francie, since the debacle, too, but everyone just acted like everything was fine. Maybe the romance with Zander would just peter out and she wouldn't have to 'dump' him.

Frankly, she hadn't given it a lot of thought; her mind had been completely consumed with thoughts of Cade. Savannah didn't know what she was going to do but one thing was for certain, the weird-warped fairly tale that was California needed to come to an end. She needed to go home and sort out her thoughts where things were normal and life made sense and it wasn't influenced by beautiful scenery, luxurious accommodations or the presence of Cade Champion.

Still, for days she wondered why Cade hadn't called. She half expected each ring of her cell to be Cade, calling to make some glib remarks about the kiss, but he hadn't - at least not until this morning. And, when he finally did call he didn't mention their hot make out session. Rather, he seemed subdued, serious in fact, but friendly, inviting her come over at chore time saying he had something to show her that he'd been saving for just the right day. Savannah didn't hesitate about saying yes. Instead of calling Zander, she left him a cryptic note saying she was taking a drive and would be back later and not to wait up. She was going to see Cade and Zander didn't need to know about it.

Cade finished his rigging, rising to his full height. Then, he just stood there and looked at her. His gaze was intense the way it always was when he regarded her - slow and thorough. Savannah's eyes met his, she didn't attempt to demure or act cute this time. She knew what she wanted and she boldly met his gaze.

"You're beautiful just like you are everyday, Savannah," he said plainly. "How about a nice warm hug?"

Savannah smiled brightly as she and Cade put their arms around each other for a long moment. He lightly rubbed the area between her shoulder blades, she breathed in his scent and reveled in the feel of his strength. "It's been four days and I have missed you every moment," Cade whispered.

"I've missed you, too."

"Here's a group of fall calving cows," Cade said, indicating the pairs. He stopped the 4-wheeler, killed the engine, and dismounted. "Thought you might like to see some of these-you haven't been through this group," he added as he opened the cooler and pulled out two beers.

About twenty-five purebred pairs were milling around in a pasture that overlooked the showbarn, but Cade was right - she hadn't seen the group and said so.

"Well, that's because they just came in from a cowherd dispersal out in Michigan. I got 'em on order buy."

"They're nice," Savannah commented appreciatively. "The group is so uniform they could all be full siblings. Are they all two-year-olds?"

"Yeah, two and three, yep. And, you're about right, that herd has been pretty closed so everything is pretty linebred."

Savannah walked closer to a cow nursing her calf, sipping her beer. "A couple of these could show!"

"Exactly, that's why I bought 'em. Pedrocelli Ranch needs some new genetics and needs to up the game if they are going to expect a lot out of these sales."

Cade stood next to her as he gazed at the group. "I told Monica and Hollis when I hired on not to expect too much this first sale and that we had some culling to do, but that we could get them where she wanted to be in a couple generations if we worked at it."

"That makes sense. This is great group, it really is," she said, taking too big of a drink and sloshing a little of the suds over her mouth.

Cade reached up and touched her lips, wiping the extra away as if his hands on her face were something he did everyday. He put his damp fingers to his lips, tasting the beer. "Mmmm, beer tastes better after it's been on your lips."

"Cade." He had finally started to relax, to act more like his usual teasing self.

"Load back up!" he commanded suddenly with a swat on her rump. "You're special surprise is up ahead!"

Savannah threw her long legs over and plopped on the seat in front of him. "Hold on!" Cade jeered as a firmly put his right arm around her waist and gunned the motor. "God, I like the looks of those legs of yours," he murmured in her ear. Savannah smiled and scooted deeper against his body.

They rode on, climbing higher into country that Savannah hadn't seen. Cade took his time, explaining that at points they crossed off of the Pedrocelli and onto a neighboring ranch and that they'd get back on the Pedrocelli land again. Savannah realized at that moment that she was happy, not just a little happy, but supremely happy, comfortable, and alive. Cade was holding her, she was relaxing into him. There was nothing in between them…

The wind picked up and suddenly and the sky, already light with bright and golden tones from the coming sunset, opened up ahead of them. She could almost smell the sea air.

"Welcome to your own personal tour of the Golden Gate Bridge, Savannah," Cade whispered against her hair.

It was far down in the distance, and at first Savannah wasn't sure what she was looking for, but suddenly, there it was, the bridge, as clear as if it was only a handful of miles away.

"Cade! This view is amazing!" Savannah jumped off the 4-wheeler and went closer to the edge of the ridge peering out with awe at the vastness before her. "I cannot believe how easy it is to see! How far away is it?" The breeze was cool and whipped Savannah's hair around.

"Oh, it's probably a good 35 miles from here, but like I said when you got to the ranch, this was the perfect day for this little treat. No fog and plenty of visibility. You can't always see the bridge from here-just on special days," Cade said, approaching her, his arms coming around her waist. Then, more softly he added. "You like your visit to San Francisco? My version is better than a helicopter or a Rolls Royce, right?"

Savannah laughed softly.

So much better he has no idea.

"I love it Cade. Its perfect."

Cade didn't say anything as he turned her toward him and pushing back long, loose tendrils, he gently kissed her lips. Savannah didn't feign resistance or try to argue a point she didn't feel, she just kissed him back, her arms looping around his neck, her belly curving into his hips.

To Savannah's disappointment, Cade pulled back. "That's enough of that for right now. I brought a picnic! Come on, let's set it up-"

"But where? It's so windy up here we'll blow away trying to-"

Cade tugged her along with him to the 4-wheeler and the supplies. "Nope, you'll see," he said gesturing to a large rock outcropping closer to the crest of the ridge. "That spot blocks the wind. Come on-you won't believe it!"

They hauled the cooler and blankets to the big rocks and on the west facing side, Savannah noticed a couple beat up lawn chairs and a grouping of stones forming a make-shift fire ring. Stepping behind the rocks, just as Cade had promised, the wind ceased.

"Somebody hangs out her on a regular basis," Savannah remarked as Cade began pulling wood from the canvas bag.

He grinned. "Yeah, this is Hollis' little hangout. He showed it to me the first week I came to the ranch. After that, it seemed like I found myself up here about every Friday night. More than a couple, I actually fell asleep!" Cade guffawed as he started making a fire. "Pop open that wine and pour us a glass," he added.

"Weren't you a little lonely up here?"

"Yes and no. I'd come here to think and I liked being alone here," Cade paused, the wood having caught fire. "Besides, I had you with me, in a way. This is where I would sit and let myself think about you as much as I wanted."

"Oh, Cade. I spent every night thinking about you, too. I thought it would quit – and I wanted it to - but it never did."

"For a while I wished I could forget you, too, maybe that was part of me taking this job all the way out here, as a way to be as far away from something I couldn't have as possible, I don't know," Cade shook his head. "But then, one day you just appeared. I swear, that first morning I saw you I thought I was hallucinating."

"Yeah, and then you surely realized that Stetson and Macy had set us up!"

Cade chuckled. "They sure did, but I'm glad," Cade paused for a moment and Savannah didn't say anything. Then he surprised her.

"I'd like to talk about your past, about the ex-husband," Cade said, taking one of her hands in his.

"Why do that? We're having so much fun. We're talking cows!"

"I know, but I want to know how you got rid of him. I almost lost you because I was too bull-headed to let you talk before. Tell me now."

Savannah sighed and began to tell him all of it - about dating when they were young, Troy always being a jerk that she felt sorry for, that he even blackmailed her into marrying him. She laughed when she shared how she and Eddie duped Troy into signing the divorce papers.

"I actually have a little more respect for Ole Ed now!" Cade admitted.

It felt so cleansing to get it all out to Cade. By the time the story was done, his arm had come around her shoulders, his thumb rubbing her collarbone softly. He had kissed her hair.

What began to happen next was natural. When Cade turned her to face him and looked into her eyes, there was not a question, just the answer. She smiled softly, her lips parted, her eyes fell closed. Cade's mouth was there, covering hers so fully he took her breath away. Their kissing was deep and sensual, sending pulsating waves of unrequited pleasure ravaging Savannah's body, radiating electricity everywhere. Then, Cade pulled back and enveloped her in a warm hug. He breathed in deeply the scent of her hair, rubbing his nose in it.

"Savannah, I am in love with you," he whispered. "Stop me now, I mean it, *right now*, because there hasn't been anyone since you. I want you so badly it hurts. I either take you back or I make love to you right now. I am past the point of being able to be with you and not show you how I feel."

Savannah faced him directly. "I didn't come here tonight for you or I to stop."

Cade let out a deep breath.

When she got the call from Cade that morning, Savannah knew that she would be with him that night - that she would *intimately* be with him. She knew that by accepting Cade's invitation to ride up to this beautiful, secluded place she was saying yes to what they both desperately wanted. She didn't know what tomorrow would bring only that she would have him again tonight. They had been careening toward sleeping together since the moment their eyes met on her first day at Pedrocelli Ranch. Savannah wanted it, selfishly in some ways; she might hurt them both after, but there was no way she was saying no to Cade tonight.

"I want you, too. Right. Now," was all it took to bring their bodies together as one again.

A look of something between relief and passion washed over Cade's expression as he kissed her again. "Remember everything that happens tonight, Savannah."

Cade didn't waste any time; he unbuttoned his shirt part way and pulled it over his head. Savannah's hands flew to his broad, brown chest, gripping wildly at the fur there he as unbuttoned her blouse, both his hands finding her bare shoulders, breasts, ribs, waist and stroking everything about her, owning her as he tasted every part of her skin as he went. Her bra was off and Cade had laid her against the blanket. He licked, tasted, smelled, and touched her all the way down to the waistband of her jeans. His fingers didn't hesitate as he opened them and with one strong arm he lifted her hips and pulled them away. Cade's breathing was so raspy and he mumbled words that made no sense. Any shyness that Savannah felt dissipated completely she needed him. As he laid her back, they both cried out with pleasure. There would not be much time, this first time together again would go so fast, but they both flew together on the shocking, consuming pleasure of coming together again.

———————— •◆• ————————

He held her under the blankets he had brought, her naked back against his naked torso. They hadn't stopped kissing yet. He would make love to her again in a moment, she knew. She needed more, *so much more*, that she was almost weak with desire. She had never felt so alive.

———————— •◆• ————————

Later, as the dusk deepened, they packed up and rode down the mountain, she on the front, Cade's coat tightly around her against the chill of the descending fog. They stopped at the showbarn, Cade walking through the calves with Savannah at his side, checking them as he always did before retiring for the night. They drove his truck the short piece to the cottage,

Savannah sitting in the middle, resting her head against his chest. He didn't speak, he just kept breathing in her hair, kissing the crown of her head.

Parked, Savannah started to reach for the passenger side door handle but Cade gently pulled her tighter against him.

"Stay."

"Cade, I should get back. All my work is over at Kingsley's."

"No." he said it simply, as if that statement were enough. Cade opened the driver's side door and slid out, pulling Savannah with him. Her feet didn't even touch the ground as he picked her up.

"Savannah, I've spent too many nights, not just since Denver, but all of my adult life, alone in a cold bed. After what we just did on that ridge, I'm not sleeping without you in my bed tonight."

Savannah complied. There was no saying no. Not tonight.

FIFTEEN
EVERYBODY HAS A PLAN

Lavender dawn began to seep across the horizon as Cade watched Savannah sleep. The way they had been together wasn't like anything he'd ever experienced. Being with her had not cured him of something cheap like lust, it had just made him need her in his life. He reached for her back, touching it lightly with his fingertips, waking her gently until she stirred and rolled to face him.

"Move in, Savannah, be with me for the rest of the week. Send someone over to get your things."

Cade smiled in the early morning twilight, but he also looked sad. Savannah shook her head.

"Cade, I have to go, I'm cheating on Zander."

That man's name when she was still naked in his bed brought vomit to Cade's throat. "Wrong!" Cade exclaimed, flinging the sheets off. "Being with him, you are cheating on me!"

"Cade -" Savannah began, but didn't know what she intended to say.

"Last night was incredible, not just some cheap thrill. I felt it, Savannah, we are still in love."

"Cade, there's no doubt, I'm attracted to you, but maybe we needed this to move on-"

Cade was furious, and deeply hurt. "I thought this could mean you were finally ready to start trusting me. Savannah, we are right for each other!"

"Why do you believe that?" Savannah's voice was elevated. "There is no reason to believe that!"

Cade relaxed and moved to sit beside her on the edge of the bed. Neither one them had on a stitch of clothing. "Because I've never felt like myself until I met you. You changed my life the moment you entered it. We're meant for each other. And yes, I believe that."

"Cade, I'm just so confused right now, I don't know what I believe!"

"Promise me you won't go back to Zander and, and – you know what I mean, I can't say it or I'll puke," Cade's eyes were full of tears.

"When I go back, I'm there to work on the book, get it finished. I'm calling it off with Zander."

"Can you *promise* me?" Cade whispered, looking relieved.

"I'm not going to bed with Zander - I'm not in love with him, but, just because of that doesn't mean I know what *we* can be," Savannah said, rising. "I just need to get home."

"It's only a couple of days until the sale. Move over here, we'll get through this, you'll finish your book and we'll figure it out!"

"Cade, I don't know if me being here for that is a good idea, I need to get home where I can think."

"We've worked so hard together! You can't miss it! Besides, Francie would be insulted."

"You're right," she smiled wryly. Cade knew her better than she wanted to admit. "I've got to get back to my own stock and I still don't have anything done about putting in embryos for next year and there's just so much else-"

Cade brightened, tentatively. "Well, actually, I solved that problem for you."

"Pardon me?"

"Yep, I solved the problem of you not having receipt cows to use with your embryos. I had a group down at the Bow String Ranch that I needed to wean and sell. When I heard you talking to Eddie a couple weeks ago, I called Clint and told him that I could help you both out. He shipped the embryos to Texas and we put them in my cows," Cade was growing smugger as his plan was revealed.

"Clint and Eddie didn't say a word to me."

"I asked them not to - I wanted to find the right time to tell you the good news myself!"

"What good news? How much do I owe you? Did Clint pay up front for those cows or what?"

"You don't owe me a thing! That's the beauty of it! We're partners!"

"Excuse *me*?"

"I talked Clint into trading a quarter interest in all the embryos for the use the receipts."

"WHAT? Cade! I cannot believe the nerve of you guys!"

"I thought you'd be thrilled and besides, this way you can't just run off and go home and stop answering my calls again. We're partners on your favorite donor cow."

Savannah was livid. Clint was a turncoat and Cade a charlatan. And Eddie, too? Savannah couldn't believe her ears.

"You three men decided what I was going to do with the embryos out of my donor and you didn't discuss it with me and yet you didn't expect me to be furious?"

Cade looked sheepish. "I guess we didn't look at it like that."

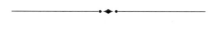

"Clint Cascade, I need to talk with you," Savannah spat into her cell phone receiver. I was at 9:30 am on the East coast, plenty late enough to call Clint.

"Savannah, I'm so happy to hear from you-"

"You might not be after you explain to me just what the hell is going on with my donor cow!"

"Oh, dear, I was wondering how soon you would be calling about that."

"Is it true, you gave Cade part of the embryos for the use of his cows, all without talking to me?"

"Uh, well, yes. Now, when Cade called me, I thought using the receipts was generally a good idea. But, I'll admit, when he said we wanted to do it without you knowing, well, I thought it might backfire-"

"Some partner you've turned out to be, Clint."

"I'm sorry about that, but I was trying to help Cade. I went along with it because Cade assured me this would be the foolproof way to win you over."

"He *what*?" Savannah shrieked into the receiver.

Clint grimaced and jerked the offending shrill sound away from his ear.

Wow, she had a temper.

"Apparently, his plans aren't materializing as quickly as he had assured me that they were."

"Apparently not! I am not back with Cade!"

"Hmmm," Clint began, a teasing lilt to his voice. "Well, in that case, if you're not interested in Cade, does that mean you are finally back on the market?"

She hung up on him.

"No time like the present," Savannah said aloud as she dialed Eddie's number next. "We'll see what he has to say for himself!"

"Hey, hey, hold on, there, Savvy!" Eddie was backing up faster than Savannah could spew angry words at him. "I didn't know anything about the fact that those two jerks didn't tell you their little scheme. Shit! I figured you had talked to them and I didn't worry about it."

Savannah started to calm down.

No surprise, Eddie not worried about something.

"Well, if you knew the embryos were getting shipped to Texas, why didn't you bring it up?"

"Because, I figured between you and your boyfriends that it had been settled. I didn't think about it."

"I wish you would have talked to me!"

"Listen, Savvy, I'm sorry they pissed you off, but I got other things to think about now, too, besides your cows," Eddie replied.

"Like what?"

"Like Crystal. She's gotten into vet school in Kentucky and, well, I'd hadn't been sure how to tell you this, but I'm going to go with her and finding a job down there."

"*Vet school*?" Savannah was stunned. "She's a student?"

"Yeah, she's been working as a vet tech here and she applied and got accepted. She asked me to go with her."

Savannah couldn't believe it and she felt more that a little guilty about her assumption that Crystal had been a stripper.

"And I bet you didn't think a guy like me could find an educated woman, did you?"

"I, uh-" Savannah hesitated. This was totally left field. "When?" was all she could muster.

"Pretty soon. We're leaving right after Christmas so she can get settled and I can look for work before the spring semester starts."

"Oh my Gosh! Eddie!"

"Its time for you to come home, Savvy."

———————•◆•———————

Savannah spent the day absolutely seething. First there was Clint, then Eddie leaving, and Cade - the biggest idiot of the group! Savannah needed to buckle down and write, but she found herself pacing and finally went for a long run. She honestly was having a hard time processing everything. In the course of twenty-four hours she'd had sex with Cade, heard that she was now in partnership with him because of the turncoat Clint, Eddie had announced that was leaving and she had no farm help. Now in a matter of days she had to finish her book, get it sent off to the publisher and somehow find the courage to break it off with Zander.

Her time in California was quickly coming to an end!

She decided to call Macy hoping that would cheer her up.

"I'm am dying to see you! We'll be in sale morning at an ungodly hour, but at least I get to spend the evening before in San Francisco, so that will be cool," Macy explained her plans for coming out to the sale.

"I'm so excited to see you, too! The book narrative is done but I've got to finish making these damn CD's of all the chapter text to send to the publisher," Savannah said.

"Got it. I'm so proud of you for this project! So, stay in and get it finished because I'm gonna be bored if I have to hang out there and wait with the guys!"

"Thanks, it's been an experience, that's for sure!"

Macy laughed. "I really can't imagine! Anyway, Stetson and Cade and that auctioneer, Woody Valentine, will be making sale order the whole morning I'm sure," Macy announced, then added, "You ever met Woody before?"

"I mean, I've heard of him, everybody's heard of him, but I don't know him. Cade says they are old pals."

"Oh yeah, they are. You'll like Woody, all the girls like Woody, but auctioneer's are that way - flirts!!"

"No kidding."

"But, one thing about Woody, he does have a sexy raspy voice," Macy said wistfully.

"Well, speaking of sexy, I need to tell you, its gonna be a little awkward when I get there over to the sale."

"You and Cade feuding? Last I heard you were getting along - a little too well for you to be dating Zander - but getting along at least."

"Yeah, well, Cade and I were together in the last few days-"

"By together, you don't mean you went out for pizza, do you."

"No, I mean, we had sex."

"My God." Macy stated, breathing out heavily. "Well, how was it?"

"Which time?" Savannah couldn't help but giggle, sharing the juicy details with Macy was just a little bit fun.

"Oh girl! How many times has this happened?"

Savannah giggled again, her stomach doing the little flip it did when she thought of Cade. "Just four, but-"

"But what?"

"That was four times in about twelve hours."

"Holy s-" Macy roared with laughter. "I'd guess Zander's out of the picture."

"*Very*," Savannah said. "But, I have to let him down easy tonight. I think he is actually more serious about me than I expected. I'm not looking forward to it."

SIXTEEN

THE OFFER OF A LIFETIME

"I have something really amazing planned, so dress up," Zander commanded when he invited her to dinner. "I'll swing up to the guest cottage about seven."

Savannah had a knot in the pit of her stomach all day while she burned the CD's of her manuscript – a submittal requirement of the publisher – and packed her fairly few things. She was nervous, but it was time to let Zander go.

Right at 7 pm, Zander emerged from his Porsche in a skin-tight vest, jeans, and a suede jacket. He was obviously up to something that delighted him. "I've got a wine making buddy with the coolest, most exclusive tasting room and little restaurant. And, its *near impossible* to get into his 'Napa Eagle's Nest' as he likes to call it, but for us tonight, I even got him to close it to the public!"

Zander was absolutely giddy. Once seated, with champagne served, he made a big show of handing her another little square *Cartier* box. Savannah's breath caught in her throat.

Oh dear Lord, surely its not a ring...

Savannah tentatively opened it and seeing the lovely diamond earrings, she nearly wept with relief.

"What, don't you like them?" Zander was confused by her facial expression. "I bought them to match the necklace and to make up for how that night ended badly."

"No, no, Zander, they're incredible," Savannah said, then chugging some bubbly she added absently, "thought it might be a ring and so-"

"Oh, were you wanting a ring?"

"No. No! It's not that, it was just that you made such a big gesture that I got worried—or, I mean, I suspected," still backing up, Savannah continued, "You've just acted like you have some really big news."

"Well, I do," Zander said as he pushed an envelope with a French address on the front across the table. "Open it."

Savannah slid out the folded letter. The top bore an official-looking French seal. It was a congratulatory letter addressed to Zander, but it was in French and Savannah wasn't certain what to make of it.

"What does it say?"

"It says I was accepted into the E'Cole- Du Vin. It's the School of Enology in Bordeaux!" Zander exclaimed, literally clapping his hands together in delight. "Savannah, I'm moving to France to start studying wine under one of the great wine consultants!"

Oh, Dear God, thank you!

Relief flooded over her. She had a free out. Her luck was amazing.

"Zander! That is wonderful news! Congratulations! I'm so excited for you!"

"There's more. I'll need to leave about as soon as harvest is wrapped up, I've already gotten an assistant wine maker at the ready – I'd been working on that in case I was accepted - but I'll need to find a place and get situated."

Savannah nodded, listening to his plans, until Zander dropped the bomb she hadn't expected.

"I'm in love with you, Savannah," he said, leaning closer and taking her hand. "I want you to go with me."

Savannah was so stunned she just laughed and jerked her hand away as if it were hot. "Zander! Don't be ridiculous. I can't go with you. I'm going home."

Zander looked disappointed.

She was no more planning to move to France than she was planning to marry him.

It would be fun to have a friend to visit in France, Savannah thought guiltily. *Macy would be over the moon!*

"Zander, I have to go home to the farm after the sale. I'm not moving to France." She did not ever answer back about the 'L' word.

"Of course, I understand. And, you can! You've already been here all fall, the farm will wait," as Savannah started to raise her hands in protest, Zander charged on. "And, besides, we'll have time to visit-I'd love to see Indiana. Once I get done with school, we can bring your cows out here, if that's what you want."

Zander has put way too much thought into this....

She tried a different approach. "Its not that what you're offering doesn't sound amazing, but," Savannah took his hands in hers and softened her tone, "Zander, its just not for me. I'm a Midwest girl and I need to get back to *my* reality. It's not like we're getting married or something-besides, you need to enjoy yourself and focus! This is an important time for you!"

Again, Zander looked crestfallen. "Just think about it for a couple days, I know I've shocked you."

"I won't change my mind, Zander. I'm going home."

———— • ◆ • ————

At the cottage Savannah stopped short of opening the door. Turning to Zander, she laid her palm lightly on his chest. She caressed his cheek and looked at him for a long moment, studying him. Zander really was a handsome man. Macy's 'Hot Wine Dude # 1' flickered across her mind, causing her to smile.

How long ago that seemed....

She kissed him long and slow. Zander kissed back, his hands circling her waist, moving to open the door, but Savannah stopped him.

It was a surreal moment. Six months ago an opportunity like Zander had just given her, especially that it was with an attractive, interesting man (with money!) that wasn't a cowboy, would have been unimaginable. Most girls would consider it a fairy tale. But, here she was, turning him down. Cade was right, she was faking it with Zander. She wondered for how long.

She had just kissed Zander goodbye.

"But maybe she thinks I'm not serious, like we should get married or something,"

"Oh, Zander, I don't think she's ready for that, Honey," Francie said with concern.

Zander had come to see his mother the next day and explained Savannah's lack of enthusiasm about his offer. He was clearly frustrated.

"I don't see why not. We need to get away! Our entire relationship has been clouded by Champion and the book and the ranch and I want to show her what we can be."

"I understand your idea, but you need to think about her position. She loves her farm, she's been gone from there for months already and feels pulled to reconnect with that," Francie explained but she could see Zander fighting the idea. "Surely you can understand some of that having women like me and especially your aunt Monica in you life. Her farm is important to her, she misses it."

"I get it, I do, but maybe she thought I needed to give her a more concrete arrangement, you know, about us."

Francie's brows knitted together. "Zander, don't push. Give her a little time to think about your offer and show her that you understand. Perhaps she'll get home, miss you, and come to visit-"

"No! That won't work! If she ends up going home, Champion will somehow be there, and I'll lose her."

"Zander, enjoy the time with her, give her a few days to adjust. It's almost the big sale event. Then, consider talking with her again, maybe trying a different approach."

Zander sighed. "I really thought she'd be excited about the opportunity to go to France. I mean, Mother, you went with Dad to England for a few years before we came back here and started the winery," Zander reasoned.

Francie rolled her eyes toward the ceiling in contemplation. Zander was not getting it.

"That's true, darling, but when your father asked me to move to England, I wasn't already in love with another man."

SEVENTEEN

ON THE AUCTION BLOCK

Savannah expected the sale hospitality tent, with the influence of both Xave and Francie to be beautiful, but the scene was over-the-top gorgeous. It looked more like a luxurious party than a cattle sale. If it weren't for the light scent of barn that prevailed and the noises of the bovine outside, it could have been confused with a wedding venue.

I bet Cade thinks this is ridiculous, Savannah mused.

Savannah felt sort of privileged just to be invited to such as event. Francie hadn't spared much expense; just the massive floral arrangements on the tables and near the auction block would have cost thousands. Ten crystal chandeliers hung in various places and the doorway from the tent that gave on to the sale ring was an elaborate entryway with hanging white lights, ribbon, and more fresh flowers. There were four bars in the process of being stocked and hundreds of logo wine glasses were being set about. Two ice sculptures, one quite obviously of a bull, the other of a cow, were mounted on raised platforms, vodka ready to be dispersed from discrete 'vessels' directly from the ice bovine themselves. A band was setting up and a wooden dance floor had been erected. The walls of the tent even had gold-framed portraits of Grand Champions past and historic farm scenes displayed in such a way that he tent had a gallery feel. Digital screens were in each corner with AV equipment so those who preferred to lounge in the tent could do so and still see the action in the auction ring. But, most wonderful to Savannah were the full-color flyers advertising the cover of her book on the Pedrocelli Ranch that were spread on all the tables - Savannah had not expected that and felt a thrill that brought her almost to tears.

I've written my first book! Savannah's joy was supreme as she touched and studied the glossy cover image.

Savannah had driven over alone, thankfully. Zander planned to come, but he had been called away by some sort of wine emergency and she was grateful for the time to peruse the event and meet up with her friends without the awkwardness.

It was time to get back to reality, just on more day, Savannah realized. The book was submitted her bags were packed. She had originally planned to spend a final night at the Kingsley Estate, but when she awoke today she just felt *done*. She loaded her luggage in the borrowed Mercedes, planning to leave it at the ranch and ride to the airport with Macy and Stetson. She even got a hotel room in town for the night. Going back, looking back, just wasn't something she wanted to do and she didn't want to face a big goodbye with Zander. By tomorrow night, she'd be in her own bed again.

Alone.

Savannah was shaken out of her reverie by Xave's voice as he rushed to her, giving her a light hug and kissing both cheeks.

"Well! I'm officially flipping out!" he exclaimed, looking flustered. "And, Oh. My. God! I've got pit sweat! Yuck! Pit Sweat, Savannah!" he shrieked and attempted to air out his shirt. Given how fitted it was it didn't move much.

"Xave, its extraordinary! No one in the show cattle business will ever have seen anything like this! It's a masterpiece," she said sincerely, trying to placate him.

"I know, its awesome-of course-but Mother! Oh Lord help me! She'll be here any moment with those people from the *Sonoma Style* magazine –really, it's just a local rag, I know, but it's my first *covered* event, you know? And, they are coming at noon. NOON, Savannah! Spirit save me! Noon! And this event is barely set up!" Xave complained, then suddenly distracted by a couple of bus boys nearby, he dashed over and grabbed one boy's arm.

"WHAT are you doing?"

"Uh, setting up, Sir," the stunned server stammered.

"Honestly! Attend to the raw bar! Now! Guests will be coming in for lunch in an HOUR!" Xave looked disgusted as he released the bus boy's arm. "The RAW BAR! NOW!"

Savannah couldn't hide her humor; Xave was the definition of Drama Queen.

"Ignorant bitches! You'd think they were working in a barn or something!" Then, knowing the truth of it, they both laughed. "You ready for a little bubbly?"

"Yes! I'd love some-" Savannah was saying when they were interrupted by an ear-piecing shriek with an Oklahoma twang.

"SA-VAAA-NAAA!" Macy screeched as the girl's embraced, rocking each other side to side.

"Macy! I'm so happy to see you!" Savannah hugged her again.

"Oh, I remember you, you're the little southern belle!" Xave cooed as he leaned in to do the two-cheek kiss with Macy. "You are just in time!" he announced as the bus boy he had signaled arrived with glasses of sparking rose`.

Xave toasted with the girls and then looked at the bus boy in irritation. "The bottle! I meant bring us a *bottle*!" he demanded as the boy skittered away, then, yelling after him: "Well, make it two now, this is half gone!" Turning to Macy he said, "Where did you get those shoes? I am in L. O. V. E. LOVE!"

Macy giggled as she and Xave exchanged fashion advice for a while before Xave was pulled away to direct his event set up.

"Well, have you seen him yet today?" Macy asked. The girls had taken a table out of the way and were catching up over the provided bottle(s) of bubbly.

"No, I mean, today is sale day. He's busy. I don't want to bother him."

"True, but he's been asking about you already this morning. Looks like its gonna be a big event with the number of trucks and trailers already here."

"I'm not sure what to say, I mean, I'm going home tomorrow and our last conversation was a fight about how he and Clint did a deal – on my cow- without telling me!"

"Men are idiots! But, come on, don't be angry, Savannah. Just say to him what you want to say. Isn't it time you did?"

Savannah nodded, contemplating it over a sip.

"You did end it with Zander, right?" Macy questioned.

"Actually, I didn't have to. He's headed to France next month to go to a wine making school, so I had a free out, but-"

"He asked you to go, didn't he?"

"Yes, and I told him no way – kindly, of course!"

Macy took a long sip of her bubbles, then reached to uncork the second bottle. "It's too damn bad! Hot Wine Dude Number One is gay and Hot Wine Dude Number Two you let get away!"

They burst into hysterics.

———————— •◆• ————————

Savannah watched as Cade entered the tent, serious and deep in conversation with Stetson and a big bellied man in a cowboy hat and snap shirt. The man must have been a good prospect judging by the way the fourth man, the nattily dressed auctioneer, Woody Valentine, catered after him. Seeing the girls, Stetson waved and made a move toward them, hugging Savannah warmly.

"Ya'll are into the punch bowl I see," he teased. Then, whispering to Savannah, he said, "You forgive Macy and me for getting you out here?"

Savannah smiled and kissed his cheek. It was hard to be mad at Stetson. The big-bellied man meandered away for the bar and Cade's eyes met hers. He leaned in and hugged her lightly. "I'm so glad you're here," he said into her hair.

"Me, too," Savannah said.

"Listen here, I don't want to be left out of a meeting this lovely young lady," drawled Woody, as he removed his hat and bowed deeply. "My, my, but you are the star of the show," he added flirtatiously as he kissed her hand. "I'm Woody Valentine."

"I've heard a lot about you, Col. Valentine," Savannah smiled.

"All of it should be good, but given this company, I'm concerned about my reputation!" Woody quipped.

"Oh, I wouldn't be at all. They say you're the best," Savannah flirted back as Cade and Stetson rolled their eyes.

Woody puffed out his chest and made a mock salute. "Well, I am known to run a snappy sale and keep my customers happy."

"You ever do one of those 'world champion of auctioneering' contests?" Macy inquired, innocently.

Woody looked stung, almost horrified. Then he recovered himself and provided the girls with a devastating grin as he amped up the 'southern' in his drawl. "Hell no! Those contests are for boys that can't land the big sales and just want to prove something. Ladies, I'm Woody Valentine. When you sell with Woody, you always get a sweetheart of a deal!"

"Okay, okay! I've had about all I can handle," Cade interrupted. Then turning to Savannah, he asked if she'd like to take a walk.

"Sure, I'd love to talk, but I was leaving you alone, I mean, it's your big day."

"Yeah, I know, but let's walk through these, see if you like how Woody and I penned 'em," he handed her a crisp new sale catalog. "I feel like we did this together, so I want to show you how it's all turned out."

Cade and Savannah ambled among the neat double-rows of pens that had been constructed with fence stakes, white hot-wire tape, and plastic handles hung as gates. Most pens held groups of three or four heifers a-piece, but a couple single pens featured special bulls to display and still several more had cow-calf pairs that would sell together. Cade made several stops to speak to people he knew or buyers wanting to ask him questions, but he always introduced Savannah, seeming to beam with pride that she was accompanying him. They watched as Monica was ensconced in a group of younger cowboys that Cade had hired in to clip and work the ring.

"Looks like Monica has a new crop of boys to play with," Savannah observed dryly.

Cade laughed. "Yep, I'm old news now. It's like she has a new freshman class that has come to campus."

"She's quite the cougar."

Back near the tent and barn, Cade grabbed her hand lightly and pulled her around the far side of the building out of sight of most cattle enthusiasts.

"Hey, it's obviously gonna get busy here and then there'll be Francie's big 'after-party', so I wanted to make sure and tell you I'm sorry about how things went the other morning. I mean about the deal I struck with Clint. I shouldn't have done that behind your back. Savannah, I *honestly* I didn't think it through - seems like I am always doing things like that."

"Cade-"

"No, really, let me explain myself. You needed the cows and I had them and I should have been more up front – I know that - but it all happened when I learned about you and Zander and I just wanted to think of something – anything - that I thought would be a way to connect us that you would like about me and not him and I thought I'd help you and, well, shit. It backfired."

"You're right, it wasn't the smartest way to go about it," Savannah agreed. Her mother's words, *'he's a man, he doesn't know he's stupid'*, came to mind. Savannah did not want to fight though, not today. "Well, I was pretty pissed the other morning, but hey, its done now and I do need the cows. So, let's get through this sale, I'll find a way to get them to my place and you and I can work something out, okay?"

"Yeah, that's a plan," Cade said, his eyes misty and genuine.

"I do have something to tell you today, too," Savannah began. "Zander got accepted to an elite wine making program in France and he asked me to move there with him."

Cade's face registered shock and pain, then he turned away, instantly angry.

Savannah grabbed his elbow gently. "Cade, I'm not going. I told you, I'm done with Zander. I'm going home."

Cade's grin was broad and he bent and lightly touched her lips with his. "So, what does that mean for me?"

"Slow down, Cowboy," Savannah said, backing away a step. "Zander will be here today and I'll be around him and I don't want to embarrass him or upset Francie – so don't you act like a jerk," Savannah admonished. "Like I told you, I need to get home and clear my head. Right now, let's just start with this cattle partnership."

———————— •◆• ————————

The Auction is on!

As Macy and Savannah found their way to VIP seats arranged in the front row, to their surprise, a white-jacketed waiter arrived and offered to bring them a cocktail.

"Well, yeah!" Macy exclaimed. "I've been to some killer events, but Francie and Xave – wow - they do it up right!"

"Do they ever!" Savannah agreed, holding up two fingers as she indicated to the waiter to bring them both a round.

Guests were starting to amble in as Woody took to the auction block. "Testing. Testing. One, two. Testing. Okay, ya'll! If ya'll will find your seats we're gonna start up this sale in just above five more minutes," he announced. "But, please don't come in here without stopping at the settlement desk to get your bidder numbers. You'll wanna be raising your hands high today on this great set of breeding stock!"

Savannah took in the scene as Cade, along with Monica, Hollis, Stetson, and the ringmen emerged from the upstairs office having completed their pre-sale meeting. She knew they would have talked about what the lots were expected to bring, whether or not there was already money on anything of the lots, and who the ringmen should look out for in the crowd to bid on certain lots. Most sales, along with the auctioneer, they would also set a floor bid for each lot, too.

Francie, looking glamorous (if only a little out of place at a cattle sale), waved from her special opera-style 'viewing box' while the *Sonoma Style* Magazine people circulated around, taking snaps shots and furiously jotting notes.

Cade moved to the chutes, shouting a few orders to the unseen crew, then came back out and stepped up on the metal gate of the sale ring, chatting jocularly with Stetson, Woody, and the guys running the gates. Any moment they'd bring in the Lot One Donor Cow and Woody would be off. The ringmen moved to their positions, flirted or winked at all the ladies they could along the way, and adjusted their belts, as if pulling up their pants and re-tucking their shirts were part of the opening act of every sale. Still, Savannah's eyes kept returning to Cade.

Damn he looks good. She knew she'd said it out loud when Macy jabbed her in the ribs and giggled.

Cade's starched Wrangler jeans were snug, the tight fit perfectly cupping the shape of his backside and thighs. He'd actually donned a freshly starched shirt, and as the evening had cooled, put on a Pedrocelli Ranch logo vest. As she watched him rake one slender hand through his sandy brown hair, she let her mind drift to the night on the ridge, a place her mind went there about 30 times a day anyway...

"Hey babe, you look great this eve," announced Zander to Savannah's surprise.

Where did he come from?

"Zander, hey, I didn't know if you were going to make it in time," Savannah managed as he leaned in and kissed her lightly on the mouth.

"Macy, so good to see you again," he added, kissing both of her cheeks.

"Sale is about to start," Savannah remarked distractedly.

"Oh, I know! I've been with mother and Xave having my photo taken for her *Sonoma Style* spread, but I wasn't going to miss this! I've got to get back to her, see you in a few."

"He's extraordinarily chipper for you having just dumped him," Macy remarked as Zander moved away.

"Yeah, I know. That's kinda strange, actually. He was pretty sullen when I told him I wasn't going to France."

"All-right then! Welcome! Welcome, to the Pedrocelli Ranch in beautiful California!" announced Woody from the block. "If ya'll would rise and remove cover we'll have the singing of the National Anthem."

A young girl emerged on the block and sang the Anthem followed by Woody leading The Pledge of Allegiance and a local dignitary offering a prayer. Monica provided a few opening remarks and offered the mic to Cade, but he demurred, saying above the crowd noise that the stock would speak for themselves.

"All-right, then boys! Bring that Lot One into the ring!" Woody bellowed as the chutes clanged, the gate opened, and a broody momma cow thundered into the ring. "All-right, what-do-ya-give-me-now?" chanted Woody as he sharply tap-tapped his gavel. "Ten-thousand! Start her at ten thousand! What-do-ya-say-now!"

"Excuse me, hold on, if you would, please," came the pleasant, but insistent voice of Zander as he crowded into Woody's space and literally placed his hand on the base of the mic. Woody was not amused. He looked at Zander as though he were a vagrant requiring expulsion.

You just don't stop an auctioneer when he's got the mic, everybody knows that, well, apparently except Zander.

Zander persisted. "I've got an announcement. I'm sorry. I didn't get a moment to do this before you started, but-" Woody, appalled, relented as Zander's voice grew stronger. "Savannah, would you come in here, please?"

The crowd was silent, surprised to see the stunt.

Cade's face looked like stone.

"What does he want?" Savannah muttered to Macy in horror as she waved Zander away nervously.

"Come on, up, Babe. Don't be shy, I want to introduce you to this crowd."

"You *have* to go, you'll make him and his mom look bad!" Macy hissed. Savannah's grip was pinching her arm. "Maybe he just wants to share some comments on the book, no one has mentioned that yet."

"I hope so."

Savannah rose and approached the ring, using the side entrance to join Woody and Zander on the block. She could feel Cade's eyes burning a hole in her back. Even the Lot One Donor Cow had relaxed in the ring and looked up curiously.

"I'm sure everyone has seen the flyers on the tables for the book about the Pedrocelli Ranch that my mother and aunt Monica commissioned. I wanted to introduce you to the lovely author, Miss Savannah Morgan," Zander said proudly. The crowd, still confused, began to clap. Woody grabbed the flyer from Zander and brandished it like a poster, eager to be back in charge. Savannah smiled wanly and gave a small wave as relief flooded through her veins.

Zander indicated the mic, gesturing for her to speak.

"Thank you! It's been an honor to work with the Pedrocelli and Kingsley families on this project," she stated and quickly attempted to step down, but Zander grabbed her arm.

"Not so fast, Savannah, I do have just one more thing I want to do before this crowd," he said. Zander began to bend to one knee as he pulled a Tiffany blue box from his jacket.

"Savannah Morgan, will you marry me?"

EIGHTEEN
FIRE IN THE NIGHT

With the sale concluded, the band struck up lively western swing. Savannah was not aware of what was happening exactly, just that she was in a haze as Zander held her arm and accepted congratulations on their behalf. The moment she could get alone in the bathroom, she and Macy locked the door.

"Well, what are you going to do now?" Macy demanded.

"Well, I didn't say, 'yes', exactly," Savannah pointed out, looking at the 3-carat rock on her left hand and leaning weakly against the sink.

"True, but you didn't say 'no' and now there is *that*!" Macy indicated the stone.

"Well, he put me in a horrible position! I'll give it back in the morning. Tonight I'm just going to try and get through it and cut out early," Savannah said as she pressed both palms against her temples. "Cade's gone isn't he?"

Macy nodded miserably. "I'm so sorry, Savannah. I saw him leave and Stetson hasn't seen him since the last lot went through the ring."

"Just one dance, Zander," Savannah said weakly. She was hoping to slip out sooner rather than later. Somehow she had to tell Zander kindly. Not tomorrow, she decided as the evening wore on, no, she wanted to go home, it had to be tonight.

"Savannah! Come on! Let's celebrate a little," Zander chided. The party was crowded, from cattle people, yes, but Francie appeared to have invited half the county and Zander invited a number of his winemaking friends and as such as spent much of the evening so far smoking cigars with them. As she allowed Zander to wheel her onto the little dance floor, her stomach lurched with nausea.

I need to lay off the bubbles…

Zander moved awkwardly for a few minutes, not accustomed to two-step. Savannah went along in a fog.

"Congratulations, Zander," came the voice of Cade Champion as he bowed deeply. Then, extending his hand toward Savannah he offered it, indicating he'd like to dance. "Clearly the better man has won the beautiful lady. So, may I dance with her with your blessing?"

Savannah was stunned, she had been certain Cade had left, but here he was, with a suspicious conciliatory expression on his face. She wasn't buying it, but apparently Zander was.

"I appreciate your good manners, Cade. And, I will graciously step aside for the two of you old friends to share a dance or two."

As Zander literally placed her hand in Cade's, Savannah started to object at his foolishness. Oblivious to Zander, Cade's expression had begun to turn from faux innocence to panther about to devour prey.

"You have a lot of nerve congratulating Zander," Savannah said, trying to be irritated at Cade's bold move, but she was so relieved that he hadn't left she almost cried.

"You thought I'd run out, didn't you?" Cade knew her too well.

"I figured, so, yes."

"I thought about it-seeing you up there accepting his proposal. What the hell are you thinking, Savannah? You just told me that you weren't going with him to Europe!" Cade's voice was elevated.

"Keep your voice down. I'm not. And, if you'd watched closely, I didn't 'say yes', I just didn't 'say no'. I'm not going to embarrass Zander in front of everyone - he caught me completely off guard!"

Cade nodded, seemingly placated at her response, but then, he wasn't. "Did you consider how humiliated *I felt* seeing that idiot down on one knee, knowing I couldn't go to you?"

Savannah leaned into him unconsciously. "Cade, I didn't even have time to think-"

"Just dance with me then," he rasped as they started to move.

The minutes passed and they didn't speak. One dance became two. The band slowed the pace and Cade's cheek came close to hers, then closer still as his left hand slid farther down from the benign area of her shoulder blade to her ribs and she let him glide it down, not pushing it away like she should, finally it rested low, far, far, too low, on her hip bone, his thumb gently rubbing the area as he lightly squeezed the side of her waist and pulled her close to him.

Two songs became three.

Savannah's breath was uneven, Cade's ragged. It was insane, but it was almost as though they were close enough to be making love right there on the dance floor right, after Zander had proposed. Savannah's stomach spun and tossed. She could feel him again, on top of her, kissing her, the place she let herself go to every single night since the moment they had come together again up on the ridge.

If it weren't for clothing, Cade would be....

He knew it, too, how close they were, how they felt as one.

"Savannah, we are so good together, nothing has ever made me feel this way, only you, I *crave you* every moment of the day," the heat of Cade's whisper against her ear was almost hot enough to burn. Savannah gasped a little and tried to turn away, but she'd had enough wine and she wanted him so damn badly. But, now was OBVIOUSLY not the time.

Maybe somehow, though, just one more time before I go back to Indiana…

"Cade, we cannot humiliate Zander, this isn't right."

Cade gently twirled her away from most of the crowd. His lips slipped below her ear lobe savoring a thick, slow bite of her neck as his left hand stroked her hip bone in a circular motion that brought her even tighter against his leg - or was it something else - Savannah gasped and tried to pull back. "Cade! We *are not* behaving like this!"

But Cade, too, had had too much wine and he was not ready to release her. Savannah had not considered how *humiliated* he had felt watching Zander propose, seeing the woman he loved blindly, overwhelmingly, nod a meek 'yes' that he knew she didn't mean. Cade had endured enough of watching her fake it with a man not his equal. Cade's expression was dark mix of anger and hurt.

"Savannah, I love you. Plain and simple and there is no way in hell I can stand the thought of you going to that man's bed tonight with that ring on your finger. It's just not gonna happen." Cade's voice had a hard edge, but his eyes implored her, begging her to be his. She met his gaze and knew what was going to happen next and didn't try to stop it. Cade's right hand reached up to cup her jawline, her face was already upturned to his and her lips already parted, ready, desperately ready, as his mouth closed around hers. They breathed together as one. It wasn't a kiss; it was two beings suddenly sharing one soul, their bodies the willing conduits. The world shut out, the sounds of people's shock, of the crowd being shoved away, the rage in Zander's voice as he plowed through the stunned partygoers…

"Champion!" Zander screamed as he reached Cade, grabbing him by the collar of the shirt and spinning him around. Zander reared back, aiming to punch, but missed as Cade quickly swayed to the side. Savannah nearly fell as the two man came to together, grappling like wrestlers.

"Lay off, Zander. It's over!" Cade yelled as Zander pulled back and this time his punch connected with Cade's chin. The dance floor had cleared, but not everyone yet saw the fight ensuing. Cade stumbled back falling right into a waiter carrying a fresh tray of shrimp cocktails. To his credit, the waiter tottered and tried to save it, but the massive tray of crustaceans and spicy sauce were suddenly airborne while people tried to shy away and avoid being splattered.

"Cade! Your ribs!" Savannah yelled as she saw Cade gripping his sides in pain and sucking air.

But Cade was angry enough to fight through the pain and he sprung like a cat at Zander, crashing into him first with a punch that knocked Zander to one knee as his eyes rolled back. "She is not yours, you fool!" he roared.

Suddenly, their fight was everywhere and it was as if Xave's party palace was literally tumbling down around them. The sound of shattering glass pierced the shocked noises of the crowd. The band had come to an abrupt down beat and paused, as enamored with the brawl as everyone else. Bottles broke and crashed like cymbals to the floor as Cade and Zander careened into the ice sculpture of the bull. The massive five-foot frozen beast slammed to the floor onto its back, its hocks splintered, a fountain of chilled vodka spewing straight up from the sheath. Partiers literally clamored with cups to catch the booze. The décor was destroyed amid bloody lips, split brows, and copious amounts of cussing. Floral arrangements were launched off of tables, spilling water and petals everywhere. The final straw, as Cade moved a one-two punch on Zander, came was Zander careened into a towering stack of logo glasses sending them splintering to the floor showering the men with shattered glass. The tent pole had taken a hard hit, too, and one side of the party palace sagged, the white cloth of the tent flaccid and draping over people as they scurried to get out from under it.

"Savannah loves me and she will never be your wife! She does not love you!" Cade screamed as he got a foothold on Zander and then pinned him down. Even down one wrist and with barely healed ribs, Cade was stronger, he had more fight in him than Zander.

Suddenly Zander went limp. Stetson was there now, dragging Cade back, but he didn't need to. It was as if the fire went out of them both. Cade touched his lip, his ribs aching bitterly. Cade knew he was cruel to have said it, to have hurt Zander in front of his family, but his own hurt was too strong not to damage the other man.

"Is that true?" Zander's handsome face was scrunched up in agony. He sat up on his knees, clutching his neck where Cade's fingerprints left welts.

"Zander, I-I'm so sorry-" Savannah was crying, Macy clutched her friend's shoulders. "I just need to go home, okay? Just need to get away from you both-"

"It is true?" Tears poured down Zander's cheeks. "Answer me, honestly for one God Damned time, Savannah," his voice was soft, but seething.

"Yes, it's true, I can't marry you, Zander."

"Do you love him?" Zander spat it out with a string of blood and saliva. "Have you loved him the entire time we've been together?"

Savannah's left hand trembled uncontrollably as she held the little rock out to Zander.

"Answer me!" Zander was angry. He glared up at her, struggling to stand.

"Yes, I love Cade Champion. I never stopped."

EPILOGUE

Central Indiana, Morgan Cattle Co.,
November 2000

S he had done it again.

She was on the porch, glass of whiskey in hand, alone.

With Eddie and Crystal soon leaving for Kentucky, she really would be alone, but Savannah was happy for Eddie. Him finding someone was a plus on so many fronts and she wouldn't have to keep figuring out ways to make enough money or feel like she was responsible for entertaining him. But of course, she now had absolutely no help whatsoever. But Savannah wasn't really brooding about that as she sat, another late fall afternoon about to fade into chilly twilight. She'd been home three days from the sale. She'd run out, Macy having driven her straight to the airport. She bought a ticket, didn't care what it had cost, and flown home at 6 am after spending a night sobbing at the airport. She hadn't heard from Cade – or Zander – and was afraid to call them.

Now, it was nearly Thanksgiving, and the late fall day had been warm, though its meager heat had waned. Savannah leaned back and she stretched her long limbs, contemplating the fact that she needed to get up and go start chores. As she sipped, she heard a low rumble, a rattling sound from far down the road that sounded like an old trailer beating against its axels the way the old aluminum could bang around on the highways.

Cade certainly needs a new trailer, Savannah mused to herself recalling that his twenty-year-old beater had seen better days…

"Cade!" Savannah's heart quickened and she leapt to her feet. "Oh my God, *Cade!*"

Her body knew that Cade Champion was near before the fact could be a reality, even a distant one.

Savannah flung herself inside the house, accidentally dropping the tumbler and stepping over it. In the bathroom, she splashed water on her face, but realized it hadn't done anything but smear yesterday's mascara and redden her complexion. She dashed up the stairs, vaguely aware of the manure trail she was leaving on the carpet. She blotted her face dry then powdered her red cheeks, pausing to touch up a couple areas, then she added another coat of mascara and some light colored lip gloss that she hoped looked natural. Brushing the tangles out of her hair, she observed that her long sleeve blouse was absolutely filthy with everything from hay-loft cobwebs to crap gobs on the cuffs. She threw it and the stained old sports bra off and grabbed the closest garments she could find-a push up bra and low-cut v-neck tee shirt that were wadded up by the toilet where she unceremoniously cast the garments aside because she'd come in a little late the night before. She, Eddie, and Crystal had gone out to celebrate as a little send off for the couple. Eddie had proposed a week earlier and Crystal had accepted. Her jeans were also pretty dirty with crap around the cuffs, but a quick look in the mirror assured her that if Cade saw the v-neck, he wouldn't notice the dirty jeans.

The moment she emerged back out onto the porch, a red Ford F-250 pulling an old aluminum trailer was pulling into the drive.

Cade Champion.

Here, in Indiana.

At her farm.

It was obvious that he'd driven all night and more; California had to be thirty or forty hours from her place. He looked rung out as he stepped from around the driver's side, his plaid shirt untucked and unbuttoned just one too far, revealing a swath of brown collarbone and chest hair.

Cade smiled, looking a little afraid, yet lithe in his panther-like way. His beautiful cobalt blue eyes looked tired and had more crinkles at the corners than usual.

Savannah had started to advance off the porch toward him, but she was just so stunned, so overwhelmed by the sight of him, that she just couldn't move.

"Savannah," Cade began, pausing a little a running his left hand through his hair and feathering it back, the move the had a way of making Savannah's insides melt.

"I heard that Eddie's getting married and moving and, well, it just so happens, I'm presently out of a job again. Any chance you could use a herdsman?"

Savannah smiled, still overwhelmed at the sight of him.

"Yeah, things aren't really going to well at the Pedrocelli," Cade continued. "Monica is mad at me for not screwing her, Zander and Francie are mad at me because, well, you know, we - you know," Cade winked at the obvious. Grinning broadly, he went on, "And then, Xave! Whew! You should have seen the way he flipped out royally when he saw the mess of the party after the fight Zander and I had. He literally flung a tray of shrimp at us!"

Savannah giggled. "No!"

"Yep, he screamed something like 'well you two bastards didn't dump this one so here it is!'"

"Seriously?"

"Yeah, come to think of it, the only person at the Pedrocelli Ranch that actually likes me, surprisingly enough, is Hollis! So, like I said, its not like I have a job right now."

"So, you're so sure of yourself that you thought driving all the way to Indiana would be a way to find work, huh?"

"Savannah, I'm not sure of a damn thing except that I love you and I'm pretty sure you really do love me. So, I just decided to get in the truck this time and drive."

Savannah threw herself off the porch and ran into Cade's waiting arms with a force so powerful that when she landed against his chest, they both fell back against the truck. As Cade's mouth found hers, the heat of the grill seared at the back of his calves, enough that he pushed them both to the fender as he enveloped her in a kiss so deep and sensual they were both consumed, without words, unable to say verbally all that was left unsaid from the last year, but spoken through the voices in the language of love.

"Cade ! Your ribs! I'm so sorry!" Savannah started to pull back remembering his fall but he smothered her worries with his lips.

"Savannah, tell me, I have to know. Do you love me?"

"Oh, Cade! How did you? Why did you - I didn't expect to see you here, I-"

"Eddie called me. He did a standup thing for once and said he was leaving and that I should probably know. And, Monica, yes, Monica, came to see me after the sale as I was packing to leave and told me I would be a total dumb ass for not coming after you."

The sound of clicking metal as the truck cooled down was interrupted by a chorus of impatient bawling from the trailer. "The receipts! Oh, Cade - you went to Texas to get them?" Savannah broke off the embrace and running to the side of the trailer, with her foot on a fender, she peered in. Twelve branded-up black cows studied her with a mixture of curiosity and complete irritation.

"I couldn't come here asking to stay with nothing at all, could I?" Cade purred as he hoisted himself up behind her and then pulled her back into his embrace. "You haven't answered me yet, Savannah, and I need to know. I've driven a long, long, way, from California to Texas, to Indiana to get one answer, once and for all. Do you love me and need me in your life?"

Savannah felt the pressure of Cade's firm body against her back and warmed to him. She knew her answer and would never be wrong about it again.

"I love you, Cade! You have no idea how much I love you!"

"Good. These cows can wait a little while longer then," Cade mumbled as he gently lifted her into his arms and carried her toward the house.

Savannah didn't know what they would do next or how it would work, but she knew one thing - she would never doubt her love for Cade again.

"I love you Cade Champion with all of my heart."

As Cade kissed her, Savannah felt more joy than she ever dreamed possible.

She had the heart of a champion.

THE END... (At least for now!)

READING GROUP QUESTIONS FOR DISCUSSION

1. At the beginning of the book, Savannah swore off cowboys and love. Do you think that is why she resisted Cade or was Savannah just acting childish by not forgiving him sooner?

2. Why do you think Savannah continued to put Zander's feelings above Cade's even though it seems she always cared for Cade?

3. Through out the book Hollis is a character in the background. Did it surprise you that he eventually supported and even helped Cade and Savannah?

4. Cade ultimately tried to go behind Savannah's back to in win her over, yet he was angry that she was dishonest with him when they first met. Do you think Cade was being a hypocrite or that he just didn't realize she would be angry?

5. Savannah has two guys vying for her attention for much of the book. Is she really undecided about who she loves or is she just enjoying the attention?

6. What do you think will happen next for Cade and Savannah? Can they make it as a couple and build a life and farm together? Should they try? Do you think that is where they are headed at the end?

7. Savannah is a strong female character but not a perfect one. What attributes do you like about Savannah and what about her makes you cringe?